DØØØ5616

Reader's Comments

"WOW! Beautiful, raw, courageous, hopeful." H. E.

"This book is a "must" read by any woman that has ever been hurt and is determined to gain strength. Even though this book will make you cry, it will also give you strength and understanding!" Dr. M. T. J.

"I highly recommend this incredibly sensitive book for any who feel like they've been taken to the very edge of despair with no way of ever returning to a beautiful life. There is hope. I had trouble putting it down and couldn't believe the depth of vulnerability shared." L. H.

"A compelling read. The stories exuded hope and joy despite unbelievably horrid, difficult, and heartbreaking circumstances. I couldn't put it down." B. G.

"These amazing women enter in as victims, but leave as victors-- redeemed, restored and whole. The emotional spectrum as I read ranged from sorrow and heartbreak for the storyteller, and absolute abhorrence and anger towards the aggressors and abusers. The end of each story left my heart soaring..." K. G.

"Although the stories are raw and real, the redemption is the takeaway. Each story highlights the way God is able to use our stories to encourage and inspire others..." T. C.

"Gripping. I could hardly put it down! I will be giving this to LOTS of hurting women, who, I believe, will identify and feel freedom through reading this." Amazon Reader

BL**OOM**
In the dark

TRUE STORIES OF
HOPE AND REDEMPTION

Paula Mosher Wallace

Ordering Information:
Quantity sales. Special discounts are available on quantity purchases by corporations, associations, and others. For details, contact the publisher at the address above.

ISBN 978-0-9965309-1-0

Bloom In the Dark, Volume I, First Edition
Printed in the United States of America
All scripture references are taken from the Holy Bible, King James Version, Cambridge, 1769

All names, locales, places of residence, physical descriptions, occupations, professional affiliations, and other identifying characteristics and details have been changed to protect the privacy of individuals and to maintain their anonymity. As such, any resemblance to actual persons, living or dead, or actual events is purely coincidental.

Dedication

I dedicate this book to all the women who shared their
stories in these pages.
You are amazing!
You have faced the worst life had to throw at you.
You not only survived your darkness,
but have relived it to share your stories with others.
Your courage and selflessness have truly humbled me.
Your testimonies demonstrate what it means to *Bloom
In the Dark*.

Table of Contents

Flower names were chosen for these anonymous stories based on the historical meanings of flowers as referenced in The Old Farmer's Almanac as shown on their website:
http://www.almanac.com/content/meaning-flowers

My soul, wait thou only upon God; for my expectation is from him. He only is my rock and my salvation: he is my defense; I shall not be moved. In God is my salvation and my glory: the rock of my strength, and my refuge, is in God. Trust in him at all times; ye people, pour out your heart before him: God is a refuge for us. Selah.

Psalms 62:5-8

EX-VICTIM

By Zinnia

I don't **want** to admit I'm a "Victim"
Tainted by abuse
Feeling irrational fear and shame
Defensive and jaded
Frigid, stoic, rude
Rejecting before I get rejected

I don't want to **admit** I'm a "Victim"
Who was too weak
To get away, to fight, to stop the pain
To stand up to the bully
Who killed my innocence
Who massacred my soul

I don't want to *be* the "Victim"
Making mistakes
That cause more abuse
Broken choices that hurt me
I end up hurting others
Instead of stopping the pain

I want to *stop* being a "Victim"
Attracting predators
Accepting abuse as my due
Putting myself at risk
Choosing to trust the wrong ones
Who just pretend to protect

Jesus, *help* me stop being a "Victim"
You became a victim for me
You hung naked on the cross
You bore my shame
You were bruised for my iniquities
By Your stripes, I am healed

I am *no longer* a "Victim"
Forgiven of sin
With wholeness of heart
Redeemed, healed and loved
My innocence restored
My soul saved

I am *now* an "Ex-Victim"
I testify of His grace
I was lost but am found
I was shattered but am restored
I am filled with relentless love
I am sharing it with others just like me

*For thus saith the high and lofty One that inhabiteth
eternity, whose name is Holy; I dwell in the high and
holy place, with him also that is of a contrite and
humble spirit, to revive the spirit of the humble, and to
revive the heart of the contrite ones.*

Isaiah 57:15

Naked On Stage

By Holly

Naked. On stage. I am a little girl--only nine. The lights are so bright, I have to close my eyes. I am facing away from all the people who must be laughing at me. I can't breathe. I'm shaking. I want to run and hide, but my feet won't move. Tears start sliding down my face. I'm helpless and ashamed.

God, I can't do this! I scream in my head. *I can't be this exposed in front of everyone! They'll judge me and make fun of me.*

Then I feel a gentle nudge. God's telling me to turn around. I picture the fancy, carved boxes people sit in. I see the gold paint and velvet curtains. This is the fanciest opera house I've ever seen. I know I can't let all those snobby, rich people see me naked and crying. Regardless, I turn around slowly. I will just keep my eyes closed and pretend they can't see me. I hear silence as I feel the heat from the spotlights.

God, please help me. I have to face them. I didn't come this far to give up. Besides, before I got here, I thought I was ready for this stage. Ready to stand for the truth in front of God and man. Ready to stop being a victim. Ready to publicly stand up to my abuser.

Peace settles over me, and I slowly open my eyes. What? The audience isn't filled with fancy dresses and suits. I blink and look again. Can it really be? Naked little girls. The audience is all naked, little girls. They are every color and size. They are looking at me with tears running down their faces, too. Their eyes are open in wonder. Wow! I can see the hope lighting up their eyes. Each little girl is realizing she is not alone in her humiliation and shame.

I can do this for them!

I remember why I'm on stage. I'm a grown woman who's been damaged and hurt since I was a little girl. I am not standing on stage in shame, but in God's strength. I start to breathe, slow and steady. I get to show all these women that there is hope. That, even though they were hurt so young, they don't deserve the abuse. I am showing my nakedness to give hope to each little girl who was molested, raped, beaten, shamed, abused, abandoned, laughed at, used, hurt. I am standing on stage telling you that you didn't and don't deserve the abuse. That God has a plan for you. That you can stand up for yourself. That you can be healed and restored.

In the pages of this book, you will read the naked truth. You will read true stories of the little girls who joined me on stage to show their nakedness so you would have hope. You will see and experience our darkest times with us, but you will also see how we made it through.

We are sharing how we saw God's hand in our surviving, healing and restoring journeys. Whether you've experienced these types of damage yourself or know someone who has, may this book speak love and compassion to you. May you reach out to the Creator of the universe for healing and restoring. Jesus hung naked on the cross, "despising the shame" to show us the way to salvation and restoration.

Why would I revisit all my pain and shame to write my stories and those of others who have lived through agonizing situations? Well, I've been postponing this project for over a year because I didn't want to remember the intense pain I've lived through. I also haven't wanted to ask other women to relive their nightmares. Nothing about this book is easy or fun. This book is about sharing our pain in order to give you hope as you walk through your crucible...as you watch your dreams go up in smoke... as you live through your abuse, betrayal, guilt and shame.

There is HOPE! God can redeem, heal, and restore you from everything imaginable. Maybe your story won't be mirrored in this book, but you will still know that our God can meet you where you are, help you survive the destruction, and give you hope for your future.

* For Paula's testimony, go to "Dear Reader" at the end of the book

Who shall separate us from the love of Christ? Shall tribulation, or distress, or persecution, or famine, or nakedness, or peril, or sword?.......Nay, in all these things we are more than conquerors through him that loved us. For I am persuaded, that neither death, nor life, nor angels, nor principalities, nor powers, nor things present, nor things to come, Nor height, nor depth, nor any other creature, shall be able to separate us from the love of God, which is in Christ Jesus our Lord.

Romans 8:36-39

Kneeling At the Altar

By Hyssop

I didn't like church. Those people who called themselves Christians were all hypocrites. They went to church on Sunday after being at my house drunk on Saturday. One thing was for sure, I never wanted to be one of "them." When Dana invited me to church this time, I just couldn't say no again.

Now, here I was bawling my eyes out at the altar at the front of her church. I wanted Jesus to save me. I started crying out a lifetime of hurt. Hurt that I had never shared with anyone. Hurt that I had locked up for so long that I'd gotten really good at pretending it wasn't there. Hurt I was feeling again....

When I was only eleven, I worked for my dad's business. We all worked to help pay the bills for the traveling circus. Even my nine year old sister, Susan, did her part. I walked into the building where we stored everything. A minute later, I heard someone come in. I wasn't worried because my dad had other people working for him, too. But then the door lock clicked. That was weird. I saw Ed walking toward me with a mean look on his face. "You can never tell anyone about this." He said.

About what? I couldn't think of anything I'd want to tell anyone. Then he grabbed me and put me on a table. As I struggled, I realized how strong he really was. He was going to hurt me somehow. I thought that I could survive anything. After all, I'd been yelled at and beaten before. Besides, if he left marks on me, people would ask about them.

"If you tell anyone, I'll do the same thing to Susan that I'm going to do to you. She's smaller, so it will hurt her worse."

Crap. I love my little sister. I'll do anything to protect her. I'd take her to the closet that we could lock from the inside, to hide, while daddy was beating momma. Whatever was about to happen, it was better for me to handle it than to risk her getting hurt. I froze as he took my clothes off and started feeling me all over. Then he took his belt off. Why did I have to be naked to get beaten? Just to make it hurt worse?

No. Instead, he was pulling his pants down. I started to panic. What was he going to do to me? I quickly found out as I felt shooting pain. He was forcing one hand between my legs while he grabbed himself with other one. I closed my eyes and went far away. I could handle a lot of pain, but this hurt in my chest. In my heart. Everywhere. I wanted to hide in a black hole and never come out.

When Ed told me to get dressed, I realized that he was done. He reminded me not to tell anyone. He said that I'd asked for it by being so sassy. He promised not to hurt my little sister as long as I let him do what he wanted to do to me and never told anyone. I was bleeding. How was I going to explain that to my mom? I'd just tell her I was starting my period. She had told me about bleeding every month. This was different, but she'd never know.

I tried to avoid ever being around Ed. Every waking minute, I was thinking and scheming of ways to get him to quit. Over the next two months, he caught me off guard two more times. Each time, I told my mom the same lie about having my period. I started my period a few months later, so she never knew.

I finally figured out how to get rid of Ed for good. I would make it look like he stole money from my dad. I waited for a day when he was closing out the registers and counting the money. After he left, I snuck in and took two hundred dollars. The next morning when my dad counted the money, I heard him yelling. I smiled as he swore at Ed and fired him for stealing. Ed tried to defend himself, but my dad was furious and wouldn't listen. I breathed a huge sigh of relief. Now, my sister and I were both safe.

Still crying at the altar, I felt someone put her arm around me. I felt love and support, but couldn't stop the thoughts or the crying. It was like I was crying out the poison that had been building up in my system for many years.

I remembered the rural school that we had to go to when I was twelve. The principal called me and Susie into his office. He told us to be quiet as he locked the door. Hearing the door lock sent me back to that mess with Ed. He went to his desk. I started shaking as I watched him pull a gun out and put it on his desk. Susie had a frozen look on her face already. She knew what was about to happen.

The principal said he'd kill us if we didn't do what he said. With that big black gun sitting on the desk, I wasn't about to try anything. He told me that my job was to watch. By this time, I knew what rape was. He made me keep my eyes open and watch him rape Susie. She was like a rag doll who knew the drill. I was torn between wanting to protect her and being thankful that it wasn't me on that desk.

When the nightmare was over, I helped Susie to the bathroom to get cleaned up. She said that no one would ever tell on him because they all believed he would kill them.

On the way home, I told my brother what had happened. I begged him to never tell anyone why, but to help us get away from this school. The next day I pretended to be sick. Luckily, my parents had decided that we needed to move to a new place anyway, so I was safe. I had always hated that we moved so often, but this time I was so thankful!

The tears kept coming as I knelt at the altar. They were dismissing the service, but I needed my new Savior to keep cleansing me of all this poison. I was married, and had two children, but everything about physical intimacy disgusted me or hurt. I just wanted it to be over. On several occasions, my husband made that worse. He was drunk and forced himself on me, even though I begged him not to.

At this altar, I finally felt loved and accepted. I felt forgiveness wash away the guilt and shame. I'd always felt like those horrible things had been my fault. Somehow, I must have caused them or deserved them. I was starting to feel clean for the first time. All those showers I had taken, trying to wash away the stain of shame, had never worked. These tears were finally washing away that sense of dirtiness and of being unworthy.

Evil was a horrible part of the world, but I now had a Savior who was shamed, beaten and killed to give me life and hope. His blood was washing me whiter than snow. I felt like his blood was erasing the stain of my blood. After a lifetime of hiding in the dark to escape the verbal and physical abuse, I felt warm light start filling my soul. I knew that this would be a journey. I knew that it wouldn't be just some sort of magic transformation. I would have to learn to see things differently. I would have to learn who I was without the constant pain and fear.

My marriage wasn't magically fixed. My situation didn't turn into "happily ever after." I loved being a mother, but I would never have gotten married if I hadn't been trying to get away from my dad's anger and violence. Now, I had a chance to see how my changing would improve my world.

I became a fixture at that altar every Sunday for the next several years. I knew Jesus would meet me there. I knew He would keep cleansing me. I knew He would put His arms around me and make me feel safe. Now, with my soul refreshed, I knew I could walk out of church, week after week, and face my future with hope.

*I will extol thee, my God, O king; and I will bless thy
name for ever and ever.
Every day will I bless thee; and I will praise thy name
for ever and ever.
Great is the Lord, and greatly to be praised; and his
greatness is unsearchable.*

Psalm 145:1-3

Free to Feel Again

By Daisy

Running through the woods
Away from myself
Away from the world
Hiding so no one will ever know--
My pain, my shame, my loss
My little legs too short to run
Fast enough or far enough
My life running down my legs
Am I going to die?

"Help" I whimpered
I wanted to shriek and scream
But no one can ever find out
He'd whispered in my ear
"Tell no one"
"They won't love you anymore"
The bleeding won't stop. Hide it!
Toilette paper, panties, over and over
Keep hiding, forever

When will the pain stop?
It hurts me to my core
My body, bleeding
My soul, shattered
My spirit, dying
He was so big and strong
Built to protect
Destroyed my life!

Little girl, now a woman?
Innocence gone
Would it show on my face?
Stop crying! Just. Stop. Now.
Seared from the inside out.
Numbness setting in····.
Never safe. Never to be loved. Ever.
Face the real world
Shut down and survive!

God???? Help!!
I've believed in You, always.
But where are You?
Please love me, anyways.
I won't tell anyone.
Protect me? No one else has.
Please be real
Don't leave me
You're all I have

I keep talking to Him, years pass
As I grow into the woman
I'd already become
He knows my name, my shame
His Book says He loves me
I know in my head, but I can't feel
My heart cloaked in shame
Frozen, dark
ALONE
Is love never to be?

Desperate for help, I confess
To those who should have known
Disbelief on their faces
How had I hidden this for so many years?
Couldn't they see?
Quietness, seriousness, numbness

Much older than my years
No joy, no laughter, nothing⋯
Hard work to earn approval
Yet never measuring up
Walls built to hide and protect
Masking the bleeding inside
I still feel alone

At church, worshiping, praying
Suddenly surrounded with warmth
Thawing the ice inside
Walls start breaking,
Feeling vulnerable, exposed
My melting heart hurts,
They don't know why I'm crying
They speak "life and healing" on the outside
But I'm on the inside
Too broken to believe

Running through the woods, again
Away from myself
Away from the world
They've thrown stones before
Judged, rejected, abandoned me
Face down, in the dirt
Defiled, naked, ashamed
A hand reaches out to me
Neither do I condemn thee

Could it be true?
Grace, forgiveness, redemption?
The tears I hid inside for so long
Running down my face
I see nail-scarred hands
Offering healing and hope
Stop running. Stop hiding.
Start embracing life!

Forgiveness, healing, joy

Now bubbling LOVE, floating

Guilt and shame lifted

Free to feel again

Hope soaring, DANCING

Sunshine, flowers

Innocent in a white dress

Alive and Beautiful

I am loved, I will be loved

I am His BELOVED!

The LORD is nigh unto them that are of a broken heart; and saveth such as be of a contrite spirit.

Psalms 34:18

Mirror, Mirror

By Coriander

"Mirror, mirror on the wall, who's the fairest of them all?" I ask as I look at myself in the mirror. I know the "fairest" will never be me. I'm not really sure what that would actually look like. I remember from a very young age, my dad making comments about women: "too fat," "big butt," "squinty eyes," "ugly teeth," etc. I really couldn't remember much about what made a woman beautiful. I did know that if you weren't pretty, you weren't worth anything.

My older sister, Betty Ann, was pretty. At least she didn't get a lot of bad things said about her looks. My dad even commented on her pretty legs. The nicest thing he ever said to me about my appearance was "your eyes are shining like a rat's." I was so broken that I actually thought this was a compliment. I mostly tried to avoid my dad's saying anything to me or about me, because it usually made my want to cry. Daddy said no woman ever looked pretty when she cried. Crying made all women look ugly. So I tried never to cry. No matter what anyone said or did to me.

As we grew up, Betty Ann, who was five years older, showed me how to act around boys. She said, "Always dress to impress. Make sure to flaunt what you've got! You can't expect men to want you if you're not showing off a little." She always had boys chasing her. It seemed like she was "in love" with a different boy every other week. I didn't really understand what she meant when she first said that "you have to put out to get a guy to love you." When I asked her, she said I'd know soon enough.

When I was twelve, I remember overhearing a conversation between my mom and dad. Dad had just listened to an explicitly sexual voice message on the answering machine. The caller explained exactly what he liked about Betty Ann's body and what he wanted to do with each body part he mentioned. I was shocked. I didn't even know what a lot of the words meant. My dad then told my mom not to be so upset. He said that Betty Ann was doing the right thing by taking care of her men. It was her job to make sure that guy felt good about himself. Women were designed to please and satisfy men. My mom shut up and deleted the message. I knew something must be wrong with this, but I couldn't understand what.

I realized that the mirror might never tell me I was fair, but that I could still try to get men to notice me. When I was fifteen, I decided to hang out with some "cool" girls at school. I was excited when a few of them asked me to go to an apartment after school where some "real men" had invited them to party. They said that Tommy had invited me, too. I'd seen Tommy around the school parking lot a couple of times and thought he must be picking someone up.

They told me he was twenty-eight and seemed to like me. I was so excited that a man wanted to spend time with me.

Tommy made me feel special. He paid me compliments and told me he wanted me because I was so beautiful. I knew he was lying about my being pretty, but I could tell that he really wanted me. One afternoon, I went over to his apartment after school without the other girls. He had told me to come alone. Wow. I must be extra special for him to want just me.

When he started telling me how incredible I was, I was willing to do just about anything. He kissed me and started rubbing up against me. He'd held my hand and given me little kisses before when the other girls were around, but this was very different. When he said he wanted to "make love" to me, I realized he wanted to have sex. I froze up. I wasn't ready for this. I didn't want to get pregnant. I was scared to say no, but I told him no anyway. He just kept kissing me and taking off my clothes. When I said no again, he said he knew I really wanted it. He told me he would make me into a real "woman." I said, "Please, NO!"

He kept going like he couldn't hear me. I had no idea what to do. My dad had said it was our job to please men. My sister acted like having sex was the only way to get what you wanted. Maybe, this was how it was supposed to be. I quit fighting. Maybe this meant Tommy really loved me. But it HURT! If this was "making love," why did it have to hurt so much?

When I went into the bathroom to clean up, I realized I was bleeding. I grabbed a pad out of my purse. At least I had that. As I washed my hands, I looked into the mirror. Was I more beautiful? I was loved and wanted. Tommy had told me I was wonderful before he let me get up. My stiff face looked frozen instead of beautiful. My hair was messed up. My lips were swollen. And I was crying. I was ugly. I rinsed off the tears and tried to smile. I didn't want Tommy to think I was ugly, too.

Over the next month, I kept "dating" Tommy. It was more like I would go to his apartment to have sex with him. He told me I was beautiful, and I craved the attention. I didn't like the sex, but at least it didn't hurt like it had the first time. I just wanted to feel like someone thought I was special. When I told Betty Ann, she was impressed that I had found a man that wanted me. Then Tommy disappeared. No one knew what happened to him. He was just gone. I was relieved.

Brent was only twenty. He told me I couldn't tell anyone about us because that could get him in trouble. I dated him for a while and didn't tell anyone. He told me I was really special and beautiful. He said that he loved me and wanted to show me how much. Sex seemed to be the only way guys could show you that they "loved" you. I wanted to hear the compliments and get the attention. I decided letting them play with my body was the price tag I paid for the love I wanted. After a few months, I broke up with him because I didn't like how I felt about myself.

I finally dated a guy at school who had been asking me out for a long time. Maybe guys my age weren't as stuck on sex as the older guys. I quickly found out that sixteen year olds wanted sex just as much. I didn't like feeling used. After sex, I felt ashamed and used. The compliments didn't mean as much anymore. I looked in the mirror and saw disappointment and regret.

I was only sixteen and already wanted to be done with men. There had to be more to life than this. I wanted to actually be special and beautiful to someone. I remembered what I had heard at church. God had created us in His image and said it was good. He knew us before the foundations of the world. I'd gotten lost in the confusion of being a teenager, but I needed something to hold onto. I looked up the scriptures that said Jesus loved me enough to die for me.

I had sinned. I was ashamed. I had disappointed God, but Jesus had died for my sins. Could He forgive me? I asked for forgiveness and felt peace settle over me. The shame and dirtiness were gone. I knew something had changed. I actually felt loved and accepted. I looked in my mirror to see if it showed on my face. I saw rosy cheeks, high cheekbones, bright blue eyes, full lips and silky black hair. That couldn't be me. This girl was glowing and full of life. Her lips couldn't stop smiling. I was plain and sad. This girl was alive and happy.

I no longer needed men to validate or accept me. Jesus was the only man who mattered, and He thought I was beautiful. I was special enough to die for. This was going to take some getting used to.

Falling

By Goldenrod

Falling
like a rock off a cliff
fear and resignation

Tumbling
through the air, out of control
nature's strongest force destroys

Panicking
emotions running wild
can I survive this

Doubting
what I once was so sure of
who God is

Shattering
my life into pieces
as I hit the bottom

Shocking
pain as I awaken
from the deepest despair

Blinding
light pierces my pupils
seeing clearly for the first time

Questioning
the prospect of trusting
I could get hurt again

Contemplating
a new life
another chance awaits

Choosing
a different path this time
no turning back

Learning

from my mistakes
to have faith again

Following

God's plan for me
healing me from this brokenness

Surrendering

completely to God's love
the greatest Force ever known

Collapsing

into the safety of His loving arms
I choose to trust

Embracing

His plan for my life
my destiny awaits

*Why art thou cast down, O my soul? and why
art thou disquieted within me? hope thou in
God: for I shall yet praise him, who is the
health of my countenance, and my God.*

Psalms 42:11

WALLS

By Honeysuckle

"The walls around you were built one brick at a time, so they will have to come down, one brick at a time. I want to love you through this process." Darren said. "I will love you whether you love me back or not." When Darren said this, I knew he was the man God had sent to me to help me heal from my broken past. He was a godly man who wouldn't let me reject him.

How had I built up such incredibly thick walls? The Wall of China had nothing on me. I had built these walls to survive. Good luck getting them down.

I thought back to that drive in the car with my granddad. I was twelve years old and was visiting my grandparents for a week. Near the end of my visit, my granddad asked me if I wanted to drive his car on the dirt roads. It was a really nice car, and I was feeling so grown up sitting behind the wheel. He sat close to me so that he could help me if I needed it. I'd started to get the hang of driving the car when I felt granddad's hand slide up inside my shirt! What?

"Stop! You shouldn't do that. How am I supposed to drive with your hand bothering me?" I said. I hadn't started turning into a woman yet and had no idea why my granddad would want to touch my chest. When he didn't move his hand, I let go of the steering wheel and pushed him away.

He had to grab the steering wheel so we wouldn't crash. He laughed like it was all a joke. A couple of minutes later, I felt his hand slide up inside my shorts and inside my panties. I yelled at him to stop and pushed him away again. I was so angry! I told him I didn't want to drive anymore and to take me home. I was so glad when he did.

When my mom came to get me at the end of the week, I told her about what her dad had done to me. She said she had no idea why he would have done something like that but that she knew I had no reason to lie. Years later, I found out that she had confronted her family and then found out that he'd done the same thing to one of my cousins. The family decided to blame it on the stroke he'd had. They said that he must not have known what he was doing.

I never wanted to see my granddad again because I felt so dirty when I thought of his hands touching me. I was furious when my mom made me go to his funeral. To me, he was just a dirty old man.

I had always felt worthless and unattractive, so I worked really hard to be somebody that others would love. I was so excited when I finally became an airline stewardess! Then, I got engaged to a successful attorney. My family wanted me to marry him. Since I'd already slept with him, it seemed like the right thing to do.

That year, I turned twenty. Valentine's Day was going to be magical. I looked forward to the flowers and chocolates. I did get a rose, but later wished I hadn't accepted it. I should have known things weren't going according to my plan when I got my flight schedule and realized that I'd be spending Valentine's Day in freezing cold New York. That was ok. My friends and I would make it fun anyways. We planned to have pizza in one of the girl's rooms. We tried not to fall asleep as we waited to check into our hotel. It had been an exhausting flight.

I was about to check in when a bellhop in uniform walked over to me with a red rose. "Happy Valentine's Day. This is for you because you are the fairest of them all!" Maybe this Valentine's Day wouldn't be so bad after all. I smiled because a man had chosen me as the prettiest of them all.

The foundations of my wall had been built throughout my childhood. I had never felt very pretty because my parents always talked down to us children. My mom was constantly critical, so I never felt attractive, much less beautiful.

After I settled into my room, I went to Veronica's room where we were supposed to meet. No one answered the door, so I went back to my room to wait for them. Back in those days, we didn't have cell phones to track each other down, so I didn't know what else to do. A few minutes later, someone knocked on my door. That was quick. The other girls must be ready now.

I opened the door to see the same bellhop who'd given me the rose. His name tag said Allen, and he was holding a tray with champagne and two glasses. I didn't know we'd ordered any, so I told him that the party wasn't supposed to be in my room but in room 130. I told him we weren't ready, so to take the champagne to room 130 in 20 minutes.

Allen said he'd rather just wait for them in my room. I was ridiculously naïve and trusting. He had been so nice to me, so I let him in. He went ahead and poured the champagne and suggested that I have some while we waited. I took a few sips while I listened to him talk about how amazing he was. He told me about how many women he'd romanced.

I should have sensed that something was wrong, but I just smiled and listened. Suddenly, the coffee from the flight and the champagne hit, and I had to go to the bathroom. I excused myself and ran to the bathroom.

I expected him to be gone when I came out, but he was still there. I picked up my glass and excitedly told him about all of my plans for the future.

Without realizing it, I was sipping my drink as I described the beautiful wedding I was going to have. But it was getting harder to think and talk. I felt woozy. I hadn't drunk enough to feel buzzed, much less like this. He must have drugged my drink!

He smiled as he pressed his advantage by trying to kiss me while pushing me down on the bed. I screamed at him to stop. I started fighting as hard as I could with the spinning in my head. I managed to get away and ran towards the door. He beat me to it and bolted it shut. Then he dragged me back and slammed me down. My head hit the marble top of the night stand. If only I'd passed out then!

"Please don't tear my uniform!" I begged after I realized I could never win this struggle. I'd had sex before, but I had never been attacked like this. As I cried and begged him to stop, I just kept hoping that I'd pass out. Just as he seemed to be finishing, I finally did. When I woke up, I was hoping that it was all a horrible nightmare. Then, to my absolute horror, I realized that I wasn't dressed and he was lying on the other bed! I yelled, "Get out of my room, you bastard! Now! I'm calling the front desk!" He casually got up and left like nothing was wrong.

I was numb with shock. I wanted to cry and scream but felt like a heavy, frozen statue. My tears were locked inside of me. I realized it was morning. Why did the girls never call? Then Veronica called my room to ask if I wanted to go shopping. I told her that I didn't think so.

When I asked her why they had never gotten me for the pizza party, she could tell something was wrong. I wasn't my usual, bubbly self. She came to my room, and I told her what had happened. She listened to my story in shock. She couldn't stop saying how sorry she was. She tearfully explained

that they had called my room to cancel, but when I
didn't answer, they figured I was already asleep.

Veronica and I decided that I needed to go to
a doctor to get checked. We found a gynecologist
nearby who could fit me in. Scared and shaking, I
entered his exam room. I managed to get into the
gown, but couldn't make myself open my legs to let
him examine me. He was so kind and
compassionate. Finally, he talked me into letting
him make sure I was okay.

He quietly told me that there was sperm and
that I would need to take a pill to make sure I didn't
get pregnant. Abortion was still illegal, so he assured
me that this was not an abortion pill. He also gave
me antibiotics and something for the nausea the
other pill would cause. I was detached. It felt like all
of this was happening to someone else.

I walked back to the hotel in a trance. This
couldn't be happening to me. I showered for a long,
long time trying to get that animal's contamination
off me. I still felt dirty. That afternoon, as I got ready
for my flight back, I realized that he hadn't torn my
uniform. It looked like nothing had happened. I
started panicking at the thought of putting that
same uniform back on.

It was the only one I had with me, so with
shaking fingers I forced myself to put it on.

I looked in the mirror and saw someone who
looked just like a wax figure of me that should be in
a museum. She had a frozen smile on her face.
Somehow, by God's grace, I managed to get ready
for work. I went downstairs. The other girls were

waiting for me. They'd heard what had happened and were furious on my behalf. They had already made sure the scum ball was nowhere to be seen.

While I was getting ready, Veronica had threatened the hotel manager with calling the police. We were contracted to stay at this hotel whenever we were in New York, so, for all our sakes, Veronica wanted to make sure that that bellhop didn't hurt anyone else. The manager acted shocked at my story, but then admitted they had had other complaints about the same man.

Veronica was furious that the hotel hadn't gotten rid of him before this happened to me. She threatened that I would file a high publicity lawsuit against the hotel if that man was ever seen by any of us on the premises again.

Despite the other girls' offering to cover for me, I worked my shift. Like a machine, I smiled and served the passengers on that long flight. I needed to be doing something so I didn't have to think about my nightmare. Unfortunately, my mind kept running through all the ways I'd been stupid and naïve. Why had I let him in the room? Why didn't I leave when he wouldn't? Why did I drink that stupid champagne?

The mental torment continued as I realized that I hadn't even reported my attacker to the police. I was afraid that I would lose my job. The airline had strict rules about letting guys into your room. I was sure everyone would think it was my fault. That I'd somehow asked for it. What was I going to tell my fiancé? I couldn't do anything to publicly embarrass him, or I'd be stuck at home with my horrible family instead of living my "happily ever after." I couldn't afford to jeopardize my job or my future to get back at my rapist. I felt stuck in a black hole of shame and humiliation. My walls continued to grow higher.

When my fiancé saw me, he could tell something was horribly wrong. I admitted what had happened. He was furious! How dare someone damage what was his! He told me to carry a knife on me at all times. He said that if "that man" ever showed up and tried anything, I was to stab him to death. As an attorney, he was sure he could get me off with a "self-defense" plea. I didn't think I could actually kill someone, but I carried that knife with me anyway. I knew I couldn't let anyone hurt me that way again.

Fortunately, I never had to see my attacker again. On our return trip, the other girls signed me in and ushered me up a service elevator so that no one would see me. When they checked me in, they found out that the hotel manager had finally fired Allen. The hotel owners didn't want the negative publicity we'd threatened. Maybe, I'd actually prevented another stewardess from getting raped.

I spent the next few months trying to forget that anything had ever happened to me. I had a beautiful wedding, followed by a short, painful marriage. I left my husband after a couple of years because I couldn't handle the abuse anymore. This added abuse reinforced the walls I had built to protect myself.

The rape added to the damage from my upbringing. After that trauma, I'd made a lot of bad choices looking for love and acceptance. I couldn't see any value in myself or any beauty whenever I looked in a mirror. I had a lot of proof that I wasn't worth much. I was just a victim of abuse.

In my early thirties, God started sending people to me who loved me unconditionally. I'd been saved as a teenager, but had never been discipled. I didn't know that I could have a real relationship with my Savior. I finally began to realize that my God loved me. ME. He loved the hurt, abused, naïve, broken, battered me. Jesus, not only died on the cross for me, but He had also sent Darren to show me true love. After two years of Darren's persistently loving me, I married him.

Now, after thirty years of marriage, I am able to openly share my past without shame or embarrassment. I am telling my story to help you understand how to stay out of risky situations. As I mentor other women, I see how my past is helping to change their futures.

I want to help all of you young women to stay safe. If it's too late for that, I want you to know that your life is not over. God can and will restore you, if you ask Him to. He is the only One who can break down your walls and help you to be open and vulnerable again. Then like me, you too, can reach out to help others.

*The Lord thy **God** in the midst of thee **is** mighty; he will save, he will rejoice over thee with joy; he will rest in his **love**, he will joy over thee with singing.*

Zephaniah 3:17

Don't Ask, Don't Tell

By Myrtle

I looked down at my ankle and saw the tattoo that represented my old lifestyle. Even with the laser treatments that were supposed to erase it, it was still a clear reminder of what God had done in my life. I smiled as I finished putting on my wedding shoes. I let my white dress drop down to cover that old faded tattoo.

The girl looking back at me in the mirror was truly happy. Her black curls were piled up on her head under the tiara and sheer veil. Could those innocent brown eyes really be mine? I wanted to pinch myself. This was definitely a day of miracles. A day I had thought I never even wanted.

The thought of marriage was not a happy one for me. When I was thirteen, my parents announced their divorce. I felt disillusioned, hurt and angry. I blamed my mom the most and quit having any contact with her. I chose to live with my dad. When I withdrew from everyone and stopped hanging out with my boyfriend and other friends, my dad got concerned. I wouldn't even participate in any afterschool activities.

My dad's solution was for me to get involved in a church with an active youth group. That is where I first met Alesha. I was fifteen, and she was one of the youth leaders. She was a dozen years older than I, but she made me feel welcomed and accepted into the youth group.

My dad was so happy that I had a friend who made me smile and act alive again, that he let me spend as much time as I wanted with Alesha. She filled so many voids in my life. When she asked me to stay with her on weekends, I felt wanted. When she asked me about my pain, I felt understood. When she confided in me about her own problems, I felt needed. I felt unconditional love from her when I wasn't feeling loved by anyone else.

That emotional bond started leading toward physical touches. I didn't realize that my codependent relationship with her would lead to a whole new lifestyle. At first, the touches didn't seem sexual. I felt like she was being an affectionate "mother." I craved that attention, so I would let her play with my hair as I watched a movie with my head in her lap. I would feel special when she would sit close to me and rub my arm lightly while we talked. Our relationship felt completely normal to me.

When I turned seventeen, she asked me to move in with her. I thought I would finally live in a home full of nothing but love. Soon after I moved in, however, I found out that she wanted more from our relationship than before. She told me that she wanted to express her love for me in deeper ways. I never wanted to lose her love, so I went along with the kissing that led to sex. I felt wanted, accepted, needed and loved. I finally belonged somewhere.

The next morning, when I woke up in her bed, I realized it had not been just a dream. I felt so guilty. I was sure that I had committed the unforgivable sin. Too late to go back now! I decided to enjoy this new life where I felt important and special.

I chose to embrace my new life as a happy lesbian with all my new friends. I wanted to belong so much that I ignored the feelings of loneliness and emptiness. In this new lifestyle, I just refused to think about how lost I truly felt. Even when my family begged me to quit being "gay," quoting scriptures to persuade me, I chose the lesbian lifestyle.

All was great for a few years. But when my girlfriend decided to move to San Francisco, I decided to listen to the unhappiness inside. I would try to change my lifestyle. I moved back home to be a good "Christian." This didn't last very long, because I was still in love with Alesha.

I was so lonely and nobody seemed to be able to help me. I couldn't find books about people successfully becoming heterosexual after knowing lesbianism. The pastor told me that attending church would fix me, but all it did was make me feel weird. I just didn't fit in. No one seemed to understand me at all.

I finally decided that I was just "born gay." I moved to San Francisco to see if I could win Alesha back. I lived in a basement apartment that a little oriental lady rented to me really cheap. I worked both at a grocery store and fast food chain to be able to pay my rent.

Alesha had already found another girlfriend named Macy. Jealous of me, Macy told me I would never be a "real lesbian." I set out to prove her wrong. I dove into the lesbian culture even though parts of it really scared me.

The crowd I hung out with this time was into drugs, alcohol and witchcraft. Everything about that time in San Francisco was dark and depressing. When a girl told me she had AIDS, but still wanted to sleep with me, I knew I was in over my head. I just wanted to die.

At twenty-two, instead of dying, I decided to join the army. That would definitely get me out of this mess. I was ready to get help wherever I could find it. The army would give me a purpose and a career.

The army didn't fix things for me. When I was twenty-three I decided to embrace my sexuality and quit fighting it. I thought, *I may go to hell, but at least I will have enjoyed life on the way there*. I wanted to settle down and have the security of a loving relationship and stable family.

When I met Stacy, I knew I had found that permanent family. She was amazing. We had everything in common. I knew she was my perfect match. She already had a daughter. We wanted a bigger family, so we decided that I would have our next child. Besides, if I was pregnant, I wouldn't get deployed. I could get out of the army.

We selected the best possible sperm donor and scheduled the next step in building our family. Our twin girls were born eight and a half months later. I felt overwhelmed being a mother, but with Stacy by my side, I could do this.

We seemed to have the perfect family of five, but I started feeling dissatisfied. With all the chores and responsibilities of daily life, we had somehow lost the romance in our relationship. But this was what I wanted, right? I needed to stick it out. Besides, how would I raise twin girls on my own?

One day, I drove down the road by myself. I started to think about "love." *What is love anyway, and why do I always seem to lose it?*

Out of nowhere, I heard a voice respond, ***I am Who you are looking for.*** Shocked, I answered out loud, "What?" I heard it again. ***I am Who you are searching for.***

I wasn't just hearing things. God was trying to speak to me. But why? After all I had done in rebellion to His Word? I had told Him to leave me alone so many times. Why would He talk to me now? Why would He even care?

At home that night, I found my Bible and started searching for the truth. Not the truth that others had told me--I needed God's Truth. I opened my Bible to Psalms 107 where David talks about God's rescuing those who cry out to Him. Would He really forgive me?

Over the next few months, I hid my growing relationship with God. I knew Stacy wouldn't approve, so I drove to quiet places to spend time with God. For the first time, I could feel His love. I wanted to spend more time with Him and get to know Him better. I felt more loved and accepted by Him than I had ever felt by anyone before.

As I was praying one day, I felt God ask me to leave my "family" and move back to Arizona, where I had grown up. I would have to trust Him, but He would restore my life. His plans were to show me a love greater than I had ever experienced. He showed me that I would have to sacrifice a lot, but that the reward would be well worth it.

I went home wondering how I could ever leave Stacy. How could I separate our children? My heart broke as I realized the pain I would cause Stacy and her daughter. I didn't want to hurt anyone. I had tried to change before and had failed miserably. What if I failed this time, too? Only, this time, I wasn't just hurting myself. Besides, even if I wanted to leave, I had no money and nowhere to go.

As I was agonizing over this decision, I felt God say to me, ***One day you will live the life I have planned for you. Then you will look back on this situation and realize that this life was worth leaving. This impossible change is possible with Me***. That gave me the strength I needed.

Then, Stacy came to me to tell me that she had been cheating on me. She said she was sorry and wanted to fix things. I told her of my plans to leave. I knew this was the confirmation I needed to pack up and move back to my hometown in Arizona.

As I stepped out in faith, I saw God provide a place to live, a car, a job, and everything else that I needed for myself and my girls. He always showed up on time, and I learned to trust Him with every day and every challenge. God held my hand and walked me through each step of this new journey. When we joined a church, our new church family extended love and support to us.

No, I did not suddenly see myself as heterosexual just because I was trying to follow God faithfully. I had only been with women and was still sexually attracted to them. I wasn't even remotely interested in men. Whenever I would see a lesbian couple, I would be jealous of their relationship. I would miss that incredible, emotional closeness that accompanied sex. I really did not like abstinence, but I wanted God more than sex.

God showed me that I had to bury myself in His Word. I had to use scripture to counter the emotions and desires I still fought daily. I copied scriptures to read when I felt weak. I carried them around with me. One day, as I was waitressing at a nice restaurant, the hostess seated a lesbian couple at one of my tables. Seeing them made me want to quit trying this new lifestyle and go back to what I knew.

Instead, I pulled out the scripture that was in my pocket and read, "For I know the plans I have for you, plans to prosper you and not harm you." Armed with God's word, I served them and kept going. I won that battle and other battles I faced because I had God's Word with me.

My relationship with God kept growing. He wasn't a religious theory or an external benefactor to me. He was faithfully there with me whether I was perfect or not. His love held me through those rough times. In fact, I'm really not sure when I stopped seeing women in a sexual way and started being attracted to men. There was no lightning bolt, I just knew that one day I wasn't tempted to ever return to the lesbian lifestyle.

I still wanted a family, but this time, I wanted the type of family God had designed when He had created the world. My daughters needed a father, and I regretted that I had prevented that by how I had conceived them. It broke my heart that they were having to pay the consequences for my choices.

After years of wanting a complete family, I decided that it must not be part of God's plan for me. God was just not fulfilling this desire. When I tried to date and create a relationship on my own, I ran into Christian men who made me realize I would rather have no man than the wrong one.

One man I dated was addicted to pornography and had even watched it on my computer when he was visiting. Another one raped me on our first date after I clearly said "NO!" and tried to fight him off. Needless to say, celibacy was looking better every day!

Then, eight years after I left my life as a card-carrying lesbian, I met Chris. The first time we looked into each other's eyes, I felt a rush of excitement. I'd never felt this way about anyone--especially not a man. After our first date, I knew this was the man God had chosen for me. He was the man who would chase God with me. He was everything I had ever hoped for from the dimple in his chin to his warm brown eyes, blonde hair and muscular build.

Five months into our relationship, I got past my fear of losing Chris and told him about my lesbian history. If he was God's choice for me, he would still love me. If not, I needed to know before my daughters began looking to him as their dad.

Still, as I started to tell him, I felt naked and embarrassed. I just knew I was going to lose the ultimate desire of my heart. Instead, with great compassion, Chris looked into my eyes and said, "You know I want to marry you, right?"

How could Chris know about my sordid past and still love me? He actually wanted to marry me? Wow, he was looking at me like I was pure and innocent. He seemed to see the seven years of redeeming God had been doing. For the first time, I really did want the wedding and the marriage it would begin.

I looked back into the mirror that was reflecting my beautiful wedding dress and smiling face. I gently wiped away my tears and asked my friend to fix my makeup. I knew relationships were a lot of work. I knew we would both have to adjust to our new family. My girls loved Chris, but they would have to get used to sharing me.

Regardless what the future would bring, I knew that my God was faithful. I knew that He loved me and my girls and had a wonderful plan for us. I knew that, with God's help, I could face anything with hope and trust that He would carry us through. Don't ask me for my testimony unless you are ready to hear me tell you about God's amazing love!

To: Dad

To: Dad, or Step-Dad, or more accurately Ex-Step-Dad

It's been six years since I moved out. I've had a chance to grow up a lot more. I don't want my past to define me, so I've gotten help dealing with it. Now, I see things very differently. I'm letting go. God's helping me choose to forgive and to love. I'm no longer the angry little girl you knew.

I want to apologize for so much:

> **I apologize** for hating you all those nights when I had to take care of the babies because you were in a drunken stupor.
> **I apologize** for loathing your laziness all those nights we went without supper.
> **I apologize** for scorning you when you yelled at me because your laundry wasn't clean.
> **I apologize** for resenting you every time you volunteered to help your friends repair their

cars and houses but refused to even fix the sink at our house.

I apologize for detesting you for spending all your money on beer and cigarettes, and then blaming Mama when our power was cut off.

I apologize for cursing you when you made Mama and us kids go with you to rescue your drowning, crack-addict friend who had driven his truck into the creek.

I apologize for despising you every time you drank while you drove us home from school.

I apologize for screaming at you those nights after you cursed at Mama because you had had a bad day.

I apologize for wishing the rest of your life would be miserable when I found out that you had cheated on her.

I apologize for praying for you to die in a hunting accident so you couldn't hurt us anymore.

I apologize for thinking about taking matters into my own hands to make sure you never came home.

I'm sorry for all you've been through:

I'm sorry that you had to go through all the hardship that I now know you endured, before you came into my life.

No one deserves to be treated the way you were.

I'm sorry that you had to grow up in a household where drunkenness and abuse were the norm.

I'm sorry that you had to experience the horrors of war that left you even more broken and scarred than you were before.

I'm sorry that you had to return home hoping to find some peace in a world filled with chaos, only to find out that the one person you thought truly loved you had forsaken you, just like everyone else.

I'm sorry that you had to have a constant drink in your hand; drinking was the only way you knew to avoid the pain of remembering what you had lived through.

I regret many things:

> **I regret** all the years that I wasted hating you. We both would have been better off if my reaction had been to pray for you instead.
>
> **I regret** not taking the time to get to know you. I refused to acknowledge any responsibility I might have had for our relationship being broken.
>
> **I regret** blaming you for ruining my

childhood, my family, my life. I was too
blinded by my hatred of you to see that you
were a person in need of love, just like me.

I forgive you now that I understand more:

I forgive you for refusing to go to my
baptism service. Now I see that you ran from
church because no one provided the spiritual
support you craved.

I forgive you for running straight to the
bottle when you got the call that my brother
had attempted suicide. Now I understand
what it's like to not know where else to turn.

I forgive you for treating my mom like a
slave. You were just mimicking what you saw
growing up. You didn't realize that it would
impact us kids, too.

I forgive you for not understanding how to
be a father. Now I know that it's because
you never experienced a relationship with the
True Father.

I forgive you for not being able to show love
to others. Now I understand how infrequently
anyone has ever shown true love to you.

I pray for you regularly:

I pray that you'll see, as I finally did, that
the way things used to be does not have to

be the way things continue to be.

I pray that you'll find the release from guilt, shame, pain, and regret that can only come from being at peace with God.

I pray that you'll be able to make peace with your other kids once you find God's peace yourself.

I pray more than anything that you'll be able to forgive me someday for all the years I wasn't a Godly example for you.

From: Morning Glory, the oldest daughter you raised

In thee, O LORD, do I put my trust: let me never be put to confusion. Deliver me in thy righteousness, and cause me to escape: incline thine ear unto me, and save me. Be thou my strong habitation, whereunto I may continually resort: thou hast given commandment to save me; for thou art my rock and my fortress. Deliver me, O my God, out of the hand of the wicked, out of the hand of the unrighteous and cruel man. For thou art my hope, O Lord GOD: thou art my trust from my youth. By thee have I been holden up from the womb: thou art he that took me out of my mother's bowels: my praise shall be continually of thee. I am as a wonder unto many; but thou art my strong refuge. Let my mouth be filled with thy praise and with thy honour all the day.

Psalms 71:1-8

Cry Out to Me

By Red Poppy

Frustration and fear deep inside
Buried beneath a forced smile
Why is it so hard to discard
The lies lying deep within
Critical whispers in the wind?
Even darkness cannot hide
The pain that I have locked inside

Hiding from lightning anger
Trying to forget what they said
Why is it so hard
To dismiss, to disregard
The words that were spoken
The darkness building deep within?
Even lying will not hide
The pain I feel so deep inside

Tornadoes of chaos churn within
Loudly speaking all their lies
I can't see the sun, and now I fear
The horrible pain; I'm captive here
There's got to be another way
To turn my darkness into light
Someone show me; be my guide
Help me find the truth inside

Tears fall down
I cry out loud
A hand reaches gently
Lifts me up from the ground
A voice calls to me, saying
You can be free
Cry out to Me. You will see
My love is all you need

Then the Voice of many waters said to me
Torrential rain and thunderstorms
Can't keep you from my love
I'll give you more
Than you'll ever need
Just call on Me, I'll set you free

Now when the tears fall down
And I cry out loud
Your hand reaches and gently
Lifts me up from the ground
Your voice calls to me; saying
Remember, you are free
You cried out to Me
You now can see
My love is all you need

Keep the Lights ON!

By Lady's-mantle

"NOOOOOOO!" I screamed as my dad threw me out the door into the pitch black night--again. I heard the latch close on the door that blocked out my only light. He was locking me outside where he had told me that "Old Scratch" would definitely get me. I scrambled up to the screen door and tried to shrink into a smaller ball. If I was small enough, maybe "Old Scratch" wouldn't be able to find me.

Then I heard him. I was sure that scratching noise meant he was going to get me! Crying, shivering, my heart pounding, I hugged my knees to my chest. With no moon to show me anything different, every little noise made me sure that the devil was coming to get me. Every time my drunk dad punished me by locking me outside in the dark, my panicky fear of the night got worse.

I was seven when my last sister got married and moved out. My mom had already died. I was afraid of my dad, but I was more afraid of the dark. Because I was afraid of "Old Scratch" getting me if I was ever alone in the dark at night, I quit sleeping in my beautiful room. The queen-sized four-poster bed, that my sister and I had shared, was no longer safe.

I moved a sofa into my dad's walk-in closet, under the row of shirts. At night, I would lock myself in the closet and put a blanket over the door so that no light would shine into my dad's room. Then, leaving the light on all night, I would huddle under layers of quilts, trying to block out the noises that would sound like the devil was trying to find me. Even on the hottest summer night, in that closet without air conditioning, I sweated under those quilts until I finally fell asleep.

During the day, I could recognize the causes of all the noises, but at night, I could only panic. Even as a senior in high school, I hid in that closet, listening to the scratching noises coming for me.

Everything got even worse on the nights with thunderstorms. My dad would turn off all the lights in the house and make me sit on the porch with him to watch the lightning. I hated the storms, but I hated the dark more. I grabbed my quilts to cover me. I somehow thought they could protect me a little. I shivered in fear, waiting for the lightning to flash so I could see if "Old Scratch" was coming across the yard to get me. I knew my dad wanted the devil to get me, because that's what he told me every time he locked me outside. Having him on the porch with me didn't help me at all.

Even after I got married and moved out, I still fought a terrible fear of the dark. I left lights on around the house at night. I had to have my husband in bed with me to be able to fall asleep. If he wasn't there, I had to have our big dog in bed with me. Having my two, six-foot tall, linebacker sons in the room next to mine didn't help at all. I couldn't be alone. I was a wife and mother and still paranoid at night.

When I got saved, I started asking God to get rid of that fear. I knew He could, but the fear continued to terrorize me.

In my fifties, I was at home with my grandson one time when the power went out. I called my sister and asked her to stay on the phone with me. We talked until three in the morning when the power finally came back on. I begged God to not let my power go off again. He answered by keeping my power on when everyone else in my apartment complex lost theirs due to a storm.

My cell phone helped me navigate this fear problem without as much embarrassment. Before I got out of my car, walked to my door, and turned on all the lights, I made sure that I was on the phone with anyone who had time to talk.

When I was sixty-three, I left the comfort of the city lights and moved to the country. I wouldn't have been able to do this on my own, but God showed me that helping Mei Ling, a "daughter" in my life, was more important than my fear. She had two children and needed me to help with them. She often had early morning or late evening business functions to attend. In exchange, Mei Ling offered me free rent in her mother-in-law apartment.

The huge house was set back in the woods with a driveway that seemed a mile long. There were

no street lights. There were no neighbors in sight, so
I always tried to get home before dark. If by some
chance it was already dark when I got home, I would
just call someone. Then, I would just stay in the car
and keep talking on the phone until Mei Ling showed
up.

I had adapted pretty well, but I had no idea
what to do when Mei Ling left for several months! I
was sixty-five, and suddenly, I had to deal with my
fear head on. One Wednesday, I stayed at church
until after dark. I knew I was in trouble when I drove
down the long driveway and there was no moonlight
shining down between the trees. The night wasn't
just dark; it was "inky" black! I tried to call everyone I
could think of, but no one was answering.

God, help me! I prayed. *It's just you and me
out here. You know I can't do this on my own. You
know I've fought this fear of the dark all my life.
Please help me conquer it! Protect me from 'Old
Scratch'! Thank you.*

I started quoting, "For God hath not given us
the spirit of fear; but of power, and of love, and of a
sound mind!" from II Timothy 1:7. Calm and peace
settled over me like a warm, protective blanket.
Suddenly, I knew I could do this. I turned off the car
and stepped into the night. There were no lights
anywhere, but I had a flashlight to get me to the
door.

I kept repeating the scripture and thanking
God for helping me to overcome this fear. I made it
around the bushes, up the stairs to the porch and
over to the front door. When I went to put the key in

the lock, I realized that my hands were steady. My breathing was slow and even. I'd never experienced this type of peace alone, at night, in the dark.

I made my way through the huge house and over to my apartment. The calm stayed with me as I got ready for bed. I had no man, no dog, no kids, not even friends anywhere around. I realized that I no longer needed those props. An entire lifetime of panicking in the dark at night had ended.

I had been faithful to obey God about where I was living and what I was doing. His gift to me was removing that fear that had tormented me for so long. Two years later, I am still not afraid of being alone at night. I live in the country, and I enjoy the peace and quiet. "Old Scratch" is gone. FOREVER!

And Asa cried unto the Lord his God, and said, Lord, it is nothing with thee to help, whether with many, or with them that have no power: help us, O Lord our God; for we rest on thee, and in thy name we go against this multitude. O Lord, thou art our God; let no man prevail against thee.

2 Chronicles 14:11

Dear Reuben

Dear Reuben,

I know you will never read this letter, but I have to tell you how I feel about your committing suicide. It's been a week now, and I just keep getting angrier. I'm beyond furious! When I think of how much our kids are hurting, I want to kill you. But you're dead. I can't even get that satisfaction, so I'm going to vent in this letter. Just maybe, God will make you read it and understand what you're putting us all through with that one selfish choice.

Let me start at the beginning. I was so young when I fell totally and completely in love with you. I would have done anything in the world to make you happy. In fact, I tried to do everything I thought would make you happy. You gave me two amazing kids. For them I'll always be grateful. You loved them both, but Zoey was always your favorite. She had you wrapped around her little finger. Landon wanted you to be proud of him, but he knew he couldn't compete with Zoey.

When did everything go so wrong? I know the sports injuries and motorcycle accident left you in a lot of pain, but why did you have to lash out at us? We got really good at tiptoeing around you so we wouldn't trigger that temper. Somehow, that wasn't enough.

I'm still not sure what caused you to drink so much and be so unhappy all the time. When you drank you got really mean. I thought I had it all figured out when I made sure you had only a few beers in the refrigerator. When I finally kicked you out, I found the empty liquor bottles. Then I understood how you were still getting mean drunk.

Fifteen years of marriage to you seemed to suck the life right out of me. I still loved you, but I was starting to break. Nothing I did was ever good enough. I nursed you through the pain and even the addictions to the pain meds. I took care of everything so you wouldn't have to. But it was never enough to make you happy, was it? I have to admit that life was easier after our divorce.

MONEY! That was a huge part of our mess, wasn't it? Where on earth did you spend the $96,000 we had set aside for our kids' college? Or the $263,000 you got from the injury settlement and the sale of our house? I know you were mad at me and wanted to hurt me by not paying me the $50,000 you owed to me in back child support. But, I agreed to drop it to $30,000 and then to $21,000 when you agreed to pay the lump sum immediately when the house sold. Then, when you spent or lost that money before paying me, I forgave you and even agreed to only $300 a month to get caught up.

When that's all you were paying me, we were so strapped that I couldn't even buy groceries part of the time. Then you asked me to settle for just a few thousand! I couldn't do that. Zoey and Landon were your children, too. They deserved help with their college educations. By dying, you got out of paying even a few semesters of that!

Ten years after the divorce, I was supporting Zoey and Mia, and providing a room for Landon when he needed it. You know, Mia is your grandbaby, too. Yes, we'd both have preferred that Zoey not have kids until she was married, but I wouldn't trade Mia for anything in the world.

In fact, we told you that you could come live with us so we could take care of you when you needed so much help. I was frustrated and angry a lot, but I never quit loving you! I would have done whatever it took to make sure you were okay.

Remember when your second wife left you and took everything you owned? I was the one who brought you the $300 from your child support check that month along with several bags of groceries. I had to make sure you could at least survive.

You rejected me and my help after that, but you wanted Zoey to do everything for you. She loved you and wanted to take care of you, but she had Mia to take care of, too. She was only nineteen. She didn't want to keep living at home, but she sucked it up to make sure she was doing the best she could for her daughter. Why couldn't you have been more like her? Why couldn't you have seen past your anger and pain?

Something in you seemed to need to control and hurt me. After fifteen years, when I finally decided you were never going to change, I left. That made you really want to hurt me. You threatened to kidnap the kids, so I married Mario. He was huge! The only man you were ever scared of, right?

Mario and I were only married for two years, but he definitely put the fear of God into you! You knew that if you ever hurt us, he would kill you. He would show up when you were around just often enough to keep you from doing something stupid. Mario might not have been a good husband, but he would have killed to protect us.

You fought your love for me by lashing out. You sent me that note last year that said you still loved me, remember? Of course, there was also the note after that saying that I was the cause of all your problems, and the one where you said you had to take antianxiety pills every time you had to write me a $300 check for back child support. That was only once a month! I should have been on those meds for the stress I went through every time I thought of your stealing hundreds of thousands of dollars from our kids' future!

You could have kept punishing me all you wanted to, but why did you have to hurt the kids? I know that you were just being selfish. I don't think you ever realized how much you hurt them. They forgave you for the lies and loved you anyway. I never trash talked about you, so when you would tell them lies about me, you hurt them too. I was not perfect, but I never claimed to be. I always told them the truth about anything I thought would help them make better choices than I had.

I was really bitter until I found God. After Jesus became my Savior, I gave this mess to Him so many times. I forgave you and prayed for you so much. I wish you had chosen Him as your Lord and Savior, too. You just thought I was trying to be "holier than thou." You just wanted to remind me about all the bad choices I had made. I admit I was messed up, too. I'm so grateful for the grace and forgiveness I've experienced.

I keep asking God to give you credit for asking Jesus into your heart as a child. The last thing you recorded on TV was a sermon. This gives me and the kids real hope that we'll see you again in heaven.

When I was helping clean out your house, I found that clock. You remember the one that we kept with us no matter where we moved? You made that for me when we were so in love. I couldn't stop crying when I saw it. I loved you more than any man, ever. Well, except for Landon, but that's different.

I wanted to be happy that you were finally gone and wouldn't be tormenting me anymore. But all I could think about was wishing you'd stayed around longer.

Wishing I'd somehow forced you to let us take care of you. Wishing you'd waited more than a week after Zoey finally started college to kill yourself. Wishing we'd figured out a way to work together instead of hurting each other. I'm wishing so many things.

After you hung yourself, I wrote a list of things I wanted to learn from this unbearable mess. Here they are:

- *Get your affairs in order so your family doesn't have more to deal with. It's hard enough for them to have to deal with the loss of a loved one.*

- *Make sure you do NOT leave anyone with ill feelings, even if you are not happy with the immediate situation or their attitude. You never know what's going to change before you see them again — or if you will at all on this earth.*

- *Do not have regrets. Know your decisions well enough to recognize if they will make you regret something in the future.*

- *Listen to that silent whisper in your soul that some people call instincts or*

premonitions. It is most likely God
prompting you. Listen and think.

o   Take that extra few minutes to give
that hug, say I love you, or just take
one extra glance before you walk
away. Even if you are upset remind
yourself "in the grand scheme of
things how much does this one little
thing matter?" The good stuff can
bring an everlasting calm to your soul.
The bad stuff can cause everlasting
grief, madness, regrets, depression,
sadness, and unsettled feelings.

o   If something does happen before you
get that "last chance," don't beat
yourself up about it. Most likely there
are a lot more fond loving memories
that only lasted a few seconds than
there are bad ones. Just because the
last memory wasn't great doesn't
mean that's the memory you hold on
to forever. Forgive yourself and move
forward, holding on to the positive
uplifting moments that defined your
relationship more clearly. Nobody is

perfect. Mistakes are made. That's
why we have grace and forgiveness.

o Do not let others dictate how you
   react to your feelings. Allow your
   mind to process the info given and
   make the choice best for the future
   and not just the present situation. If
   you need to cry, cry. If you need to
   show love, show love. If you need to
   walk off and regroup, then do it. You
   cannot control your feelings; however,
   you can control how you act upon
   those feelings.

o You cannot control how other people
   feel and usually not how they act. Do
   not have negative reactions to
   someone else's negative actions.
   Instead, try praying until you can
   react positively. You never know what
   is on their mind. You may be the one
   that breaks the barrier walls they've
   built up due to other's actions or
   reactions. "Think before you speak"
   — not easy, but necessary for your
   inner wellbeing and possibly other's,
   too.

o *Never expect people to understand how you feel because they probably never will.*

o *Pray for everyone, not just the people you like. Most importantly, pray with a passion for the people you love.*

o *If you have cared deeply for someone, know that you always will. You may not realize it, but true love does not go away. It may be buried in the archives of your emotions, but it is still there.*

o *Do not take everything to heart. Take whatever happens through your thought process before you let it get to your heart. People say and do some nasty things when they hurt. Pain will make people do things that will hurt other people. Whether they mean to or not, it happens.*

o *No human is exempt from life's challenges. We all have specific experiences that have molded us to be who we are. Some people just handle it better. Again, choose to act and*

react positively no matter who or what
surrounds you. God is the only Saving
Grace, the only One to impress, the
only One we truly need.

○ You are never alone — make
absolutely certain you are surrounded
by the presence of God and not the
devil. You're NEVER ALONE —
choose wisely!

Wow, this has gotten a lot longer than I
planned, so I just want to finish by saying I forgive
you--for everything. And I'm thankful. You gave me
my greatest joys in our children and now,
grandchildren. I hope you are finally free from all of
the pain, physical and emotional, that you suffered.

You'd be so proud of our kids! Zoey has
been acting so grown up despite dealing with her
pain and anger. She's working, going to school, and
loving her beautiful Mia. She and Landon have
helped each other through this mess. She's handled
your legal affairs like a mature adult. I'm so
unbelievably proud of her! You would be too. Who
would have guessed that she'd be so
strong with parents like us!

We will all hurt at some level every time we think of how you died, but, in the middle of everything, we are all choosing to be stronger, more loving, and kinder to each other. That's what Landon said at your funeral. He just wants you to be proud of them.

You know, writing this letter has really helped me. I don't feel angry anymore. God has brought good out of even this.

Be at peace,

Willow

Breakthrough

By Black-eyed Susan

Here we go again, I thought as I drove to my daughter's school. Her substitute teacher had slapped her face in class for not paying attention. The teacher got fired immediately, but I was having to go meet with the Department of Children's Services about the mess. *When will we Lentz women quit being punching bags? Now. That's when.* I thought back through the choices I'd already made to stop this family curse. It wasn't just the women, either. We were good at marrying men who had a history of abuse. We were the poster family for "Hurt people hurt people."

Both of my parents and their parents experienced traumatic childhoods. My dad came from an extremely abusive family. His earliest memory is of his dad holding a knife to his mom's throat and her begging for her life. My mom's stepdad would often beat her until she was unconscious. The pattern was obvious.

Our family didn't discriminate on types of abuse, either. Verbal abuse set the stage for the other types of abuse. When my dad was angry, which was often, he would call us fat cows. We were stick thin. When I was six and didn't know any better, I cried when I got hurt. My dad's response was to tell me that my face looked like "a chicken butt" when I cried. I quit crying then and tried to never cry again.

If being stoic and tough was what he wanted, I would learn to be that. I desperately wanted approval. I made myself shut down. *Don't feel anything.* I would lecture myself. I would become just as tough as my dad. *Show no emotion. Don't be weak.* Of course, I never got his approval. But I didn't get bullied as much, so I kept refusing to feel anything.

The physical abuse was called "discipline" when it was aimed at us kids. In a rage, dad would grab our hair and smash our heads together. We didn't seem to know how to be good enough, so he would beat us with his belt or a huge switch from outside. One night, when I was on the phone after dad told me to get off, he ripped the phone out of the wall. Then he grabbed me by my hair and threw me across the room. Out of nowhere, my older sister showed up and punched him in the head. They fought long enough for me to get away.

After a family battle like that, he would mope around the house for days, not speaking to anyone. He would just sit around and pout with this dark shadow seeming to hang over him. Everything that he did was somehow our fault. That's all we'd ever known, so we believed him. Even when we had done nothing wrong, he was able to twist situations around so much that we would start to think we were actually in the wrong. My mom, my sister and I were all confused and terrified. He was a master manipulator. He was a bully who was bigger and stronger than all of us, so he always got his way.

One night when my dad was beating mom up, she yelled at me to call 911. Shaking, I quickly dialed the number. It worked, because he quit beating her to grab the phone away from me. But then, he smashed my head into the side of the piano. That really hurt!

I heard him sweetly tell the dispatcher that he had a delinquent teenager who needed to have the "fear of the law" put into her. He asked them to send an officer. When the cops showed up, I had to listen to my dad tell lies that he seemed to actually believe.

My battered mother hid in their room while I listened to a lecture about obeying my parents. I couldn't really focus on what they were saying because my head hurt so much. My dad was obviously above the law and could get away with anything.

One day, after a beating, I was so afraid of going home after school that I went to a friend's house instead. When I told my dad that I wasn't coming home, he called the cops and had them arrest me at my friend's house. I was horrified, but I showed no emotion when they hauled me off to juvenile jail for the night.

I wasn't sure which was worse, home or jail. Being stuck alone for four hours with a huge, tattooed linebacker slanted things against the safety of being in jail. Supposedly, that should never have happened, but after that, I thought I was better off just trying to avoid the abuse at home. At least I knew how to survive that.

Where was God in all of this? Well, a twisted, abusive "God" was shoved down our throats by the Pentecostal cult my dad had started following. He took us to church every Sunday to show us off as the perfect Christian family. It was so confusing to have the "strong Christian man" be so mean and hurtful at home. He had a wonderful reputation at church and in the community.

His reputation was extremely important to him. We knew we had better never say or do anything to make him look bad, or we would be severely punished. My dad's habit of twisting scripture to justify his actions and his being such a hypocrite really damaged my relationship with God. It was a long process for me to develop a real relationship with my loving Father God.

When people would tell me what an amazing father I had, I would just smile and nod. No one would ever believe what we lived with at home. For example, one day I forgot my uniform for work. I hated going home, but I had to stop at the house after school to quickly change. Trying to avoid being late to work, I ran into the house. Uh oh. I had just burst into a Bible study my dad was having with some church friends.

I was horrified that he would yell at me. Instead, his face lit up. He invited me into the middle of his prayer circle, telling everyone what a godly daughter he had. I was too afraid to say I was going to be late for work, so I stayed for over an hour as they prayed in tongues. When my dad told me I had to pray, too, I made something up that I hoped sounded good enough that I wouldn't get punished later. I ended up getting written up for being two hours late for work.

Mom always told us that we had it easy, so I figured that it couldn't be all that bad. She would say that we had no idea what it felt like to be beaten or hurt. Sometimes she would tell us that we were spoiled rotten. Knowing we'd get severely punished, she would still tell on us to our dad. She was so terrified of him that she would do this to deflect his attention away from herself.

For over twenty years, my mom worked a full time job and handed my dad her paycheck every week. She was not allowed to have any money, because money would enable her to leave. I know she loved me in her own way because she stayed with him until I turned eighteen. Since I was the youngest, she moved out the same day I did. The only person she told where she was staying was her mom, who understood and wouldn't betray her. It was a full two weeks before my mom dared to come out of hiding.

In my late twenties, I finally found a man who could really protect me from my dad. LeBrone was a huge, black body-builder with a shaved head and a beautiful smile. He was twice my dad's size and he loved me. I believed LeBrone would protect me from anyone ever hurting me again. When he would hold me, his strong arms would make me feel safe. LeBrone seemed to be one of the genuine guys. He'd been abused as a child, too, so we had a lot in common. We were going to help each other heal and be stronger.

My dad's fear of LeBrone was a huge bonus. After our wedding, however, I found out they had a lot in common. Over the next six years, I learned that they were both verbally and physically abusive. LeBrone was addicted to alcohol, drugs and other women.

After seven years of marriage, when my husband started being abusive in front of our daughter, I left him. I had told myself that I would never do what my mom had done. I would not raise my children in an abusive home. I regretted staying as long as I did. I had stayed, hoping my husband would change.

I started reaching out to the God, Who I had been told actually loved me. I also started going to counseling. I wanted to provide a loving home for my daughter. I wanted to raise her in a healthy, loving environment. God started showing Himself to me as a God of love and healing.

I started softening enough to feel again. I had to feel the bad things and do a bit of crying, but I also got to feel the good things. I was able to let myself feel emotions. More importantly, I could trust others enough to show my emotions to them. I no longer had to be the toughest person around.

A setback in my journey to recovery happened when I tried to have a relationship with my dad after my divorce. Since I'd changed so much, I guess I thought he was different. My daughter and I went to a party at my Dad's house. When my dad asked me if he could spank my daughter if she disobeyed, I froze and didn't answer. I was still afraid of making him mad by saying he couldn't spank her, so I just ignored the question.

I bit my tongue a few times when he made ugly comments to me. I was trying to "honor" my father, but then my daughter did something foolish. I watched in total shock as my dad grabbed her and spanked her severely. As soon as the shock wore off, I ran over and picked her up. She was devastated at the anger and pain aimed at her. I held her close and ran out of the house to our car.

I left and haven't spoken to my dad since. I realized that I had to forgive him, but I still needed to stay away from him. He wasn't capable of a healthy relationship. I pray for him, but I will not subject us to his abuse. Hurt people hurt people. I need to be healed so I don't pass this heritage on to my daughter.

Through counseling, divorce care at church, and talking with other true Christians, I'm starting to tap deeper and deeper into my emotions. The numbness is being replaced with intense feelings of both pain and joy. I'm learning to give God my anxiety, rejection, shame, and guilt. I'm learning that there is hope for me.

God is near to the brokenhearted. He is nothing like the abusive, controlling "God" that my dad portrayed. God is showing me that He loves me.

I am worthy of His ultimate sacrifice on the cross. I am worthy because God created me and loves me as His beautiful daughter. His validation is the only one that matters.

My life will break through the generational curses of abuse in my family. My daughter may face a few hard things in life, like the mess with the substitute teacher at school, but they will be the exception, not the rule. She will see God as a loving Father. God is bigger than any problem we face. He can heal and restore us from any damage. As we look to Him, God will help us win the battle in our minds. He will give us the validation we need. He will help us end the generational curses. We will be the ultimate BREAKTHROUGH!

Through God we shall do valiantly: for he it is that shall tread down our enemies.

Psalm 60:12

You're not Alone

(Song Lyrics)

By Blue Salvia

It's not an easy road to travel all alone.
The burden is too heavy for us to bear.
But God has sent us one to travel by our side,
To be our acting guide, to make the burden light,
To teach us how to fight – and how to win!
Jesus...

Chorus:
So give yourself to Him. Give Him your all.
You will not fall. He'll hold you up.
He'll share your cup. He'll bear your load.
As He foretold... He'll be your all.
Just hear His call – and hasten to obey.
He'll show the way. You're not alone.

He'll take your filthy rags and in exchange
Will clothe you in His righteousness.
He knows your pain. He knows your fears,
Your hidden tears, your secret sins
You just need Him, to make it right.

Jesus…

Substance Abused

By Spring Crocus

I lay on the floor pounding my fists, crying and screaming at God. No, I wasn't a little kid. Here I was, in my fifties, pitching a fit because I was so angry and hurt. I had to let it out somehow. I had just kicked my husband, Dave, out for the last time! We'd been separated off and on, but we had never actually finalized a divorce.

Dave kept saying that he was getting clean and wanted to come home. I loved him. I wanted him back more than anything, but I couldn't deal with the drug abuse or the "other" women that came with the drugs. I'd taken him back countless times, just to be hurt more.

Today, I had taken the final stand against the drugs, lies, and damage. I was furious that, once and for all, I'd had to evict the person I loved the most. It hurt so much!

My life seemed to be a recycling nightmare. It started when I was a little girl who had to clean up the vomit from her drunk dad.   He was the only parent I had after my mom died. I lived alone with him after my brother and sister moved out.

Daddy was mean and said horrible things to me when he was sober, but he only hurt me physically when he was drunk. I never knew if he was going to beat me or get his gun. The beatings were always for some random thing. I would try so hard not to make him angry when he was drunk. But he was drunk so often, and I just wasn't perfect enough to avoid the razor strop or the belt or whatever object was handiest.

Sometimes when he was plastered, Daddy would tell me that he wanted to die. Since there was no one to take care of me, he said that he'd have to kill me before he killed himself. He'd stumble off to get his gun, and I would run to my sister's house to hide. With his gun, he would follow me to her house. She wouldn't let him in. Since I couldn't take any chances, I would sneak out the back door. I would run to my brother's house for the rest of the night.

My sister was too afraid of Daddy to call the police, but she would talk to him through the door to distract him. Eventually, he would calm down and go back home. The next day, no one talked about what had happened. I went home early in the morning to do my chores. Daddy never seemed to remember trying to kill me the night before.

When my dad was at the bar or consorting with some random woman, he was gone. I felt safe, but I had a hard time enjoying the break. All I could think about was what he would do when he got home.

Focusing my time and attention on school, I was a straight "A" student. Since no one in my family had ever graduated from anything, I was considered "strange and uppity." The culture in our part of Mississippi didn't invest much in education, but I needed to succeed at school to make me feel like I was worth something. Though my family never acknowledged my accomplishments at school, I felt like my good grades made up for some of the abuse.

I managed to graduate from high school with honors. I was inducted into the National Honor Society. Even then, none of my family came to support me. Finally an adult, I could escape this horrific situation.

Along came my "knight in shining armor"--or so I thought. When I married him, I was so grateful to get away from my nightmare at home. The honeymoon period was cut short as I quickly learned that I had married a younger version of Daddy. Out of the frying pan and into the fire I went.

I dodged his abuse as much as I could while I lived through two pregnancies. I had a boy and a girl just a year apart. They became my world. They actually loved me and looked to me for everything. I loved being a mom.

I didn't know what to do, since I was no longer his only victim. I had two children I needed to protect. I felt so guilty when I couldn't stop my husband from kicking my son to the other end of our long hallway. I didn't know how to stop him from swearing at and severely punishing my kids. I didn't know what to tell my kids when, out of pure spite, their dad took their best friends from down the street to the carnival instead of taking them. I didn't know what to tell my neighbor when she told me that my husband had slept with her fifteen year old daughter.

After thirteen years of marriage, I couldn't take his abuse anymore. I filed for divorce. My kids and I were going to be fine. We were all tough.

I'd accepted Jesus into my heart as a teenager, but I hadn't thought to ask Him to get me out of my mess. I had only asked Him to help me survive my mess. As far as I knew, this was just the way life was. I thought everyone's home was like mine. I didn't know life could be any different until my second husband came along.

Dave had been my neighbor for a long time. Though he was ten years younger, he had been in love with me for years. We were friends, and I felt very safe with him. He went to church, sang in the choir, and was different from anyone I'd ever lived with. The only drawback to marrying him was that he didn't like my kids. He had his own three kids who lived with their mom most of the time. Either he didn't like kids at all, or he just didn't like anyone else's kids.

Regardless, Dave loved me and that was what really mattered. I married him and soaked up his love like a sponge. God was finally giving me all the love and joy I had not experienced until now.

We were inseparable, especially after both of our kids graduated and moved out. We spent every available minute together. We rode our tandem bike for hours. We hiked and canoed. This closeness made the damage and betrayal so much worse when it happened.

After twenty years of marriage, the bottom fell out of Dave's world. First, he lost his job. Then his twenty-two year old daughter committed suicide. We got temporary custody of her three year old son. Dave finally went over the edge when we lost custody of her son to the other grandparents.

All this in such a short time period made him turn away from God. He quit singing in the choir, quit attending church and eventually started to drown his pain in drugs and trashy women. Working to support our family, it was a while before I realized what was happening at home.

When I came back to reality, I realized that I was still lying on the floor. The tears had dried on my face. I was drained and just wanted to hide in my imaginary pool of green jello. It was such a peaceful place to go. The light softly filtering through the trees shading my pool bathed me in calmness. In my hiding place, no sound or danger could reach me. As I thought about being surrounded by cool, cushioning jello, I finally dozed off on my bedroom floor. When I woke up, I truly gave all my pain and frustration to God. I was stubborn sometimes, but I always turned to Him in the end.

God had sustained me since I was a little girl. Over the years, I had been able to minister to others because I understood the pain they were experiencing. I knew that His saving grace had healed me. I didn't judge or look down on others when their lives were a mess because I knew I had made my share of mistakes. I learned to depend solely on God. People might disappoint and hurt me because of their own pain and abuse, but God never would.

Ten years later when I was sixty-five, I was at another Bible study. I always seemed to be at a Bible study or prayer meeting. This time, a missionary was explaining the Holy Spirit to us. When he asked who wanted prayer, I asked him to pray for me.

As he prayed, I felt all the pain and shame drain away. Like heavy weights, the fear and pain had kept me depressed for so many years. I thought that was what I deserved. I knew God said His yoke was easy and His burden was light, but I'd never felt that. Since the abuse had been there all my life, I thought it was normal.

Suddenly, for the first time in my life, I saw myself as a beautiful little girl. In my vision, my red curls were bouncing in the sunlight. I was wearing a white dress and dancing in a meadow carpeted with wildflowers that were the colors of the rainbow. I could feel my heavenly Daddy watching me with pride. As I danced, I knew I was His most treasured daughter.

The next time I looked at myself in the mirror, I saw the older version of that little girl looking back at me. Now I know that behind the wrinkles and grey hair, I am a beautiful daughter of the King. No one will ever be able to steal that from me!

I Just Want a Baby

By Sweet Pea

It had been three years—seems like such a short time to struggle with infertility. For me, it seemed to go on forever. Each month, for 36 months, I felt like I was riding a roller coaster of expectancy and hope. That high was always followed by a mad rush down to the negative test result.

As the saying goes, *hope deferred makes the heart sick*, but I wanted the version where *pregnancy makes the stomach sick*. No. It wasn't funny. Before I could grieve adequately, I had to climb the next hill of hope. I knew I had to keep my emotions positive if I wanted to get a positive result.

I knew of God, yes. As a matter of fact, I had walked with Him quite a bit in my youth. But I had forgotten God, time and time again, throughout my adult life. I hadn't involved Him in this fertility journey other than the basic, *Please, let me have a baby*.

But that didn't stop God from drawing me to Him. I remember suddenly becoming interested in Christian sermons on my car radio. My commute to work was long enough to begin learning a lot about God while I drove. I had no idea the amount of wisdom God was pouring into my soul.

On that Thursday afternoon in February, I found myself wailing in despair over yet another negative pregnancy test. Specialists in Dayton and Columbus had said that I would never conceive without medical intervention. They had intervened so many times. Fertility drugs, surgeries and painful procedures had all ended with no baby.

I had started dreading baby showers. How could those women just pop babies out? Everyone else just seemed to get pregnant whether they wanted to or not. I would make a great mother. I started to wonder, *maybe God doesn't want me to be a mother...*

As I drove home from work that afternoon, I prayed, *God, please tell me. Please. Do You even hear the prayers of a sinner like me? I'm so hurt and frustrated right now. I really want a baby. Do You want me to adopt? Maybe You don't want me to be a mother at all. I just know that, no matter what, Your plan for my life is so much better than what I could plan. I just need to know what You want me to do. Please, please, don't let me lose my faith.*

The problem was that I didn't understand God's forgiveness. I remained bound by criticism. I was convinced that I needed to be perfect for Him to even consider accepting me. Oh, how I had the Gospel so backwards!

I finally got home. With tear-stained eyes, I walked into my house past Dave, my husband, who was standing outside talking to his best friend. I had just sat down to do some paperwork when my phone rang. It was my grandmother's best friend, Angela. She had never called my house before, but she wanted to tell me something. She said, "Becky, I was praying for your family today, actually, for your uncle, Wade. But God gave me a vision of you, pregnant! Becky, He wants you to keep your faith. He is going to give you a baby."

Chill bumps ran down my arms. I ran to Dave and said, "Dave! We're going to have a baby!!" He just looked at me like I was crazy and walked away.

Doctors told us to take a break from fertility meds. Our reproductive endocrinologist said we'd get back to them after my body rested. Three months passed. My birthday was coming soon. It was Friday, May 14th, and my birthday was Tuesday, the 18th. I decided to get up that morning and take the pregnancy test that needed to be taken Monday; I could go ahead, see the negative result, cry if I must over the weekend, and enjoy my birthday without that negative result ruining my day. Imagine my surprise when two lines appeared on the stick!

We were pregnant! Despite the doctors' claim that I needed medical intervention to conceive, no doctors had been involved. God had kept His word. He had healed me. He has since blessed us with three children. But, these precious miracles weren't the sweetest gift. The sweetest gift, to me, was knowing that my Heavenly Father loved me and heard my prayers. He listened to me, in all my mess, and loved me anyway. That's the God we serve.

Behold, God is mine helper: the Lord is with them that uphold my soul.

Psalm 54:4

Choosing Life

By Iris

Two blue lines on a pregnancy test. My test. I suddenly feel like throwing up! There is absolutely NO WAY that I am pregnant! Yes, I know how the test works, and I know how people get pregnant-- this is definitely impossible. But the two lines stay there in bold blue. I'm thirty.

As a single mom already overloaded with sole custody of four kids and a full time job, I absolutely can't handle anything else! To top things off, people at church will think I'm just one of those loose divorcees. How on earth did I get here?

I think back to my resolution six weeks before.....

I'm quitting men. Period. I am not going to date them, marry them, or even be friends with them anymore! I am done being hurt by them. Ok, so I've said this a few different times already, but this time I really mean it. In fact, I've let all my male friends know that I'm not going to be friends anymore. No more romantic dates, platonic dates, or male friends "just hanging out."

Men don't really want me and my kids. They just want whatever they can get from me. I'll justbecome a "man hater" and be much better off.

With that settled, I pack up for a seminar out of town. My job is sending me for four days to learn skills that will make me more effective at my job. I like to travel and learn new things, so this trip is a wonderful break from my "real" life. I get so worn out working sixty hour weeks and raising my four kids on my own. I love them dearly, but this time away from them is going to feel like a relaxing vacation.

As I head out on the three hour drive, I get a call from Jim, one of my male friends. He just wants to make sure he understands what I mean by "not seeing" him anymore. We talk for a while. I suddenly realize that traffic is getting heavier as I get close to my destination. I'd better get off the phone and set my GPS to give me directions. What? I've been talking to him for two hours? So much for not being friends.... I end the call saying "Goodbye, for real this time."

The sun is going down as I check into the hotel where the convention is being held. It is beautiful. I have stayed here before, so it feels familiar. As soon as I have my luggage in my room, I head out to get some food. I'm alone, but I can do this. After all, I've got God with me. This works great until I'm in my room, getting ready for bed.

Then it hits me. My heart aches with loneliness and tears start running down my face. Last time I stayed at this hotel, my husband had come to stay with me for the night. We'd driven to the beach to walk in the moonlight. It was so beautiful that we'd driven around until we found a store selling blankets. One of my last happy memories with my husband, before our divorce last year, was that night, making love on the beach in the moonlight.......

All alone at the hotel, I go to sleep crying into my pillow. I wake up tired and discouraged. Through my certification classes, I do my best to stay awake. I am thankful when the intense day is over. One of my classmates invites me to join his group for supper. It's a group outing—not a date. I really don't want to spend the evening alone again. Besides, I'll offer to be the designated driver. That will definitely keep me and everyone else safe, right?

I introduce myself to the guy sitting next to me. Shawn's got a stocky build with average, nondescript features. He's not really my type, but we find out we have a lot in common. He's really funny, and I desperately need a laugh. Everyone else already knows each other, and he seems goofy and harmless, so I decide to hang out with him.

After a dinner with a lot of drinking (I didn't drink) and laughter, I drive everyone back to the hotel so we can walk to the local hangouts. The laughter and craziness increases exponentially as the drinks keep coming from the karaoke place, then the live music bar, and the frozen drink bar.

Over five hours, I've had a couple sips to taste a special drink, but not enough to count as even half a shot of anything. Shawn is being really crazy after a long series of drinks. I decide to walk him back to the hotel before anyone gets hurt.

Even though Shawn's very drunk, I feel safe. He's made a variety of suggestive comments during the evening, but when I've said "no", he's said "I respect that" and backed off. Throughout the evening, he's proven that no matter how drunk he is, he's still listening and respecting what I say.

As we slowly walk the half mile, Shawn starts to tell me about his ex-wife and kids. He still loves his ex and hates hurting his kids with the divorce. He tells me how they met and got married. Then he tells me why he left her.

Earlier, he seemed like such a tough guy, but now he has tears running down his face. (Let me be honest here, I am an absolute sucker for a sensitive guy pouring out his soul.) He's hurting, and I completely understand. I've been betrayed, rejected, and lied to. I am hurting, too.

I don't move away when he puts his arms around me. I so desperately want the attention and affection. We're standing on the dock outside the hotel, looking at the water. The moon is beautiful and gives a romantic glow to the evening.

I don't want to go into the hotel. I don't want to be hurting and alone again. I just want strong arms around me, making me feel warm and protected. What's so wrong about this anyway? We're both single. It makes sense for us to be comforting each other.

Then, he asks me if he can spend the night with me. I pull away and remind him that I'm not having sex with him. I will only do that after our appointment with the Justice of the Peace. He laughs and reminds me that I've only told him that a million times already. He just wants to cuddle. He promises to stay fully dressed. He just doesn't want to be alone with all the pain.

I feel the same way. I suddenly don't care that I've sworn off men. I don't care that he's drunk. I don't care that I might be putting myself at risk. All I care about is keeping those strong arms around me. I can pretend for a few more hours that someone cares about me and wants to be with me.

We head to my room. On the elevator, I ask myself what I'm doing. Then, I rationalize how I deserve some comfort. I've been having a horrible time with tons of stress at work, four kids, loneliness... I'm exhausted from trying to do everything. I just want to have someone hold me for one night. No one will ever know. Besides, it's not like I'm going to have a night of wild sex—just cuddling, right? I'm strong enough to make the right choices.

We climb into the bed where I'd cried myself to sleep last night. He pulls me close and wraps his arms around me. Wow, this feels amazing. When his hands start to wander, I move them and remind him that he agreed to behave. He just says that you can't blame a guy for trying and stops.

He tries this a few more times during the night with the same results. I just keep telling myself that the comfort of being held is worth the nonsense from him being drunk. I really want to believe that he actually cares about me.

When my alarm goes off, I roll over and realize it's morning. Uh oh! I'm not alone. He quickly pulls me close to him and tries to kiss me. I turn my face away, but I don't get up. I want attention. He wants to play. He says he understands the "no sex" rule, but there's a lot of fun to have without actually having sex.

I desperately don't want to be alone, so I go along with the touching and kissing. Then I realize he's apologizing because he's too drunk to perform. He's not getting hard and is evidently frustrated by this. I am suddenly grateful. I know my limits and it is getting difficult to stand my ground on the "no sex" decision. He can't force me to do anything really bad because he can't get his body to cooperate. That's a relief.

Then I realize that he's pushed my clothes aside and is trying to insert himself into me. What? I try to push him away but he's a lot bigger and stronger than me. It's not working for him because he's still not hard. I finally get him off of me and get to the bathroom.

I look in the mirror and feel like I'm looking at a stranger. This can't really be me. Not the "me" that swore off men! I almost got raped by a drunk guy I'd brought up to my room! I'm just relieved that God protected me from this getting really bad. When I finally leave the bathroom, I am so glad to see he's gone.

God, I'm sorry for my stupidity. I'm sorry for not trusting You to help me with the loneliness and pain. I didn't mean to sin against You. Please forgive me and help me make better choices. Thank You for protecting me from my own bad decisions. I'll never make that mistake again! I promise.

I put my makeup on a little heavier to cover up my feelings. Then, I paste a smile on my face and head to class. I just can't pay attention. All I can think about is needing to talk to Shawn about what happened. That's crazy. Why on earth do I want to talk to him again? He would have raped me if he could. Yes, alcohol affects people's behavior, but really?

I stop fighting myself and decide we'll have a blunt discussion when I see him again. Then I will feel better and can forget this entire episode of stupidity. Now that that's resolved, I start paying better attention in class.

I see Shawn at lunch and tell him I need to talk. He has a confused look on his face, but says he'll have time during the afternoon break. When classes let out, I find him and tell him this conversation needs to be private. We head out to the car deck. I start by telling him that I forgive him.

Now, he's really confused and tells me that he can't remember anything from the evening before. He just knows he woke up once with a headache, took medicine, and didn't get back up until lunchtime. He asks me what he's done that needs forgiveness?

Oh no, this was awkward enough to start with. Now, I'm going to have to tell him what happened? How embarrassing can this get? I start by telling him how crazy he'd acted at the bars. Then, I tell him about our conversation on the dock.

He looks at me with a shocked look on his face and tells me that he's never told anyone about his feelings about any of that. He says he'd swear I was lying to him except that it's all the truth. I'm telling him exactly how he really feels about his situation.

"But why are you forgiving me? What did I do? It's bad, isn't it? Wait, can we go somewhere where we can talk sitting down? My head still hurts a lot." he asks.

We've come this far, I might as well tell him the rest of the story. He knows I'm telling him the truth. I can't think of anywhere else to tell this embarrassing story, so I take him back to my room. I know this is crazy, but despite everything, I feel completely safe with him. He looks like a lost little boy who's in trouble with his teacher. I am blushing as I start to tell him the rest of the story. I've only gotten to the early attempts to play when he gets a horrified look on his face.

"I'm still married. We've just been separated for eight months. I've never cheated on my wife! Did we, actually, you know?"

Now, I'm shocked! This just got a lot worse. He's married? Last night he'd clearly said he was divorced and talked about his ex. Really flushed now, choking on the embarrassment, I tell him the rest of the story. He starts apologizing and tells me that he has no diseases and that he's had a vasectomy. At least pregnancy is off the list of possibilities.

I tell him again that I forgive him and that I've already asked God to forgive me for my part in the mess. He tells me that he no longer believes in God. That he had been an elder in his church and wanted to follow God with all his heart, but that the mess with his wife made him turn his back on God.

"I can't believe in a God who allows all the tragedy in my life or in the world. I've had everyone try to change my mind, but nothing will change how I see things now. There is no God. If He exists, I don't want to follow someone who lets so much bad happen." His voice sounds a little sad, but also firm and resolute.

I ask him if I can tell him my testimony. This is really insane. I'm trying to convert the guy who almost raped me? Yes, I'm crazy. Wait, maybe I'll wake up and all of this will be a dream? No. This is really happening. He says he owes me so he'll listen, but it won't change anything.

I spend about an hour telling him about all the brokenness in my life and how God's carried me through it. About the sexual abuse as a child, the abuse in my marriage, the abuse at work. The betrayal and condemnation from those I'd trusted at church.

"God has carried me through everything. He's been faithful to heal and restore. He's helped me forgive and move forward. I've had to repent for my sins, but He's always loved me. No matter what!

God's been the only one who's never left me or forsaken me." I tell him that I may have consequences for my choices, but that God's already forgiven me for failing Him.

Shawn asks me if he will have consequences for adultery from what happened between us. He left his wife because she was with another man, but now he's realizing that he's just as wrong. I tell him that if he repents for leaving God and for any sins, God is always faithful to forgive. That he should forgive his wife and try to fix his marriage.

He tells me that what I've said has gone deep. He promises to take time to think about it and possibly make things right with God and his wife. Issue resolved, right?

Like waking up from a dream, I realize that I'm still in my bathroom holding a positive pregnancy test. Shawn is the only man I've been even remotely close to in nine months. The timing of that trip is right, but it's not scientifically possible! You can't get any closer to an "immaculate conception" than that!

What is everyone going to say? I'll lose my reputation as a godly woman. (Now, I'm getting mad. If I'm going to have to wear the "scarlet letter," it's not fair that I didn't at least get a night of fun out of it first.)

I can barely afford to take care of four kids. There's no way I can support a new baby's expenses and childcare on top of everything else. I could give this baby to a couple who really wants one and can provide a wonderful family for her. That sounds good except that it will be obvious I'm pregnant, and everyone will judge me. My head hurts. If I keep this baby, I'll lose everything.

As tears run down my face, I finally understand how people can even consider abortion. Then no one ever has to know how badly you messed up. Your life just goes on. At this stage, it's just tissue anyway, right?

But after miscarrying baby Andy two years ago, I know I could never abort a baby for any reason. Before I found out I was pregnant with baby Andy, I'd taken medicine that warned its side effects included fetal abnormalities or fetal death. I've had to deal with the guilt that I might have unknowingly killed my baby. I know Andy's in heaven, but losing him still hurts too much.

I need help, but who can I trust with this? There is no way ANYONE will believe my story. If I hadn't lived it myself, even I wouldn't believe it. So I call my best friend, Tory, who'd helped me through my nightmare divorce. She has never judged me.

Once I say it out loud, it will be more real. But, I'm about to explode! When she hears the tears in my voice, she calmly tells me to spill it! Shaking and crying and making no sense, I blubber through my story. She figures out that I'm pregnant, that Shawn is still married and will not be in the picture, and that I'm panicking.

Tory calmly tells me "This can't be an accident. Only God creates life. God must want you to have this very special baby. You can do this. You are the strongest woman I know. You are a survivor.

God will help you figure out a way to make it work. If anyone rejects you over this, I will beat them up. No, seriously, they obviously never really cared about you anyway. Besides, you know how much I love cuddling babies. I'm excited. I'm going to get to hold a brand new one again." She keeps encouraging me until I stop crying.

I realize that Tory's right. If God has given me this baby, He will help me take care of her. God's never abandoned me before, why would He abandon me now? I will make whatever changes I need to, moving forward, to take care of the little life inside of me. This life is precious. I get off the phone resolved to keep my chin up and give God all my worries.

When I start thinking about telling people, I have mild panic attacks, so I talk to my counselor. She recommends that I not tell people until I've seen the doctor and made sure the pregnancy test is accurate. So I push it all to the back of my head. I take prenatal vitamins and make sure I'm not doing anything that could be harmful to my baby. I even get really creative at not drinking alcohol when at business functions or parties where I'd be expected to have at least one drink.

The doctor confirms that I am pregnant, but schedules me to come back in a couple weeks for an ultrasound to make sure the baby's okay. My last miscarriage has him a little concerned. I tell my sister, Shamala, but ask her not to tell anyone. She isn't shocked about my pregnancy because she'd had a dream that I was having another baby, a beautiful little girl. I cry. I've been crying a lot. Must be the hormones.

I'm not telling anyone else until I'm sure about a due date for a healthy baby. Those two weeks drag by, but I will finally get to see my baby's heart beat! The doctor does the ultrasound himself. I don't see a heartbeat, but I'm no expert. I ask him if everything is okay. He pauses and tells me that the baby is too small to see a heartbeat. Maybe I have my dates wrong? I promise him there was only the one time. He schedules me for another ultrasound in a week to see if anything has grown. I'm in shock. Could I be losing this baby, too? But I've already decided she's worth changing my entire world for. I've been praying for her, talking to her, looking at names for her.

God, please let me keep her! I can't bear the pain of losing someone else I love. I've already lost too much!

By the time I go back to the doctor, I know something isn't right. I've started cramping. The ultrasound still shows no heartbeat. I go home, sick to my soul. When I tell her, Shamala offers to go to the doctor or hospital with me. I have an appointment in two days.

By that time, I'm cramping and bleeding. The doctor makes sure I'm not at risk for complications and sends me home with a prescription for pain medicine. Shamala and I are both crying. She'd lost a baby before, too. I should be relieved, but I'm too devastated to feel anything but physical and emotional anguish.

God! Why would you give me a baby against all odds, just to take her away? She was going to be my miracle baby. I was willing to sacrifice everything for her! Now what? I know You have a purpose and plan for everything, but I hurt too much to even care!

I decide that Shawn deserves to know about the baby. I wasn't sure what to do before, because I didn't want to cause problems for him if he'd gotten back together with this wife. But now, I need to share this loss with the only other person who knows how this happened.

After our long talk, Shawn and I agreed not to communicate anymore; but I have his work number, so I call it. I'm shocked when he answers. He says he's in a meeting, but that he will call me after work. When he finally calls me back, I tell him about the baby.

Shawn's shocked and quickly reminds me about his vasectomy. I explain that there were no other possibilities. I also tell him that he doesn't have to worry about child support or anything because I'm miscarrying.

Shawn responds, "I am so sorry about all of this. I guess I need to go back to the doctor to get checked. I definitely don't want any more kids. Oh, and you really need to become a Christian Counselor! Before I met you, I had so many people try to persuade me to change my life, but I wouldn't listen to anyone. But after talking to you, I went home and completely changed my life. I'm really sad about the baby and sorry you are hurting, but thank you for helping me get back on track!"

Facebook pictures confirm that his family is together and smiling like they really love being together. God has taken a horrible mess and brought life out of it. I also know that I want to keep choosing life in every situation.

I look in the mirror and this time I see the "me" I want to be. I'm still single, but I'm appreciating my four children more than ever before. We are a team that does everything together. I've learned to play and enjoy life without needing a man to somehow make it better. I am a daughter of The King and precious in His eyes.

*Nor height, nor depth, nor any other creature, shall be able to separate us from the **love** of **God**, which **is** in Christ Jesus our Lord.*

Romans 8:39

My Choice

By Forget-me-not

Numb inside and out
Anesthesia blocking the physical pain
Denial blocking my emotions
I lay in my hospital bed
Refusing to think about
What has just happened

Everyone said it was just tissue
No life on its own yet
An unwanted growth
Inconvenience personified
With a husband I no longer love
Better to end things now

I don't care or feel anything
For something that never existed
Better not to live in this abusive world
Wishing I was never born either
I wouldn't have been abused
Or hurt or abandoned

Then I find my Savior
He was abused, hurt, abandoned
FOR ME
Forgiving my sins
So that I can be reborn
Making me whole

I want to share the love
The hope, the redemption, the joy
With my family
To give them life worth living
Praying for everyone
To find the meaning and purpose in life

Realization dawns on me
"It" wasn't just tissue
A person, a life, a spirit
Uniquely designed before the world began
By a loving God who can heal
Any damage the sinful world can cause

What had I done in my selfish daze
Taking a life
Murdering an innocent baby
Who needed me to love and protect
Helpless and defenseless
Remorse, Regret, Conviction

Jesus, forgive me
My selfishness stealing sacred life
Love and protect
My baby, now Yours
Please give me another shot
At giving life a chance

Five blessings here on earth
I've snuggled close
One treasure in heaven
I'm longing to meet
God's unfailing grace is now my choice
I am forgiven and loved

Thou wilt keep him in perfect peace, whose mind is
stayed on thee: because he trusteth in thee.
Trust ye in the Lord for ever: for in the Lord Jehovah is
everlasting strength:

Isaiah 26: 3-4

I'm not Bipolar

By Marjoram

I remember receiving the diagnosis of bipolar disorder. I was a wreck and had been for many years. I was mostly depressed, but also giddy at times. I was either up high or down low. Since I had my first daughter, I had left my nursing job. Now, I was a stay-at-home mother, and my children needed me to be healthy.

Before my diagnosis, my doctor had placed me on antidepressants, but the larger the dose, the worse the symptoms seemed to become. After I was diagnosed, he told me that high doses of this drug were counter-productive for patients with bipolar disorder. All I know is that when they changed my prescription, I finally calmed down.

I might have calmed down, but I also lost my zeal for life. My favorite cousin was the saddest about this. Sure, my mood swings were in check, but I was numb. She didn't like how withdrawn I was. I didn't, either. But this was better for the children, right? Somehow, I kept putting one foot in front of the other to keep my family going.

I thought about all the miracles that God had performed in my life. I had grown up exposed to Him, but had chosen a life far from Him. Still, He never gave up on me. God wooed me and loved me no matter what. He drew me back into a relationship with Him. I thought about how He had healed me of cancer. I'd definitely already gotten more than my share of miracles for a lifetime.

One day, my mom and I were sitting on her sofa while my three oldest children attended preschool. She put on a television show my sister had recorded. The TV host was interviewing a street minister who would walk the streets, pray for people's healings, and watch many people get miraculously healed. This was not a show my mom typically watched, but we were both quickly drawn into it.

As I watched the healings, I quietly thanked God in my heart. *Lord, please heal people watching this show who need it. I don't need healing today, but thank You for healing me of cancer and so many other things already.*

The Holy Spirit responded to my heart, **You do need healing of bipolar disorder.** And in that very instant, as the minister on the recording prayed for the television audience, he seemed to look me directly the eye and said, "For bipolar disorder, for schizophrenia, I command you to let them go now, in Jesus' name."

A shock of electricity ran up my arms and from my head to my toes. I went to the bathroom to be alone for a minute. I prayed, *God, what just happened? Did You really heal me? Could I be healed through a recorded television show? Of course I could. God can work through anything. But did that really just happen? Or am I deceiving myself? I hadn't planned to be healed of bipolar disorder, but did You have that planned today? Oh, God, I don't want to be a doubter, but I do want to be wise. Please show me, Lord. If You really did just heal me, please let me know. Please give me some sort of confirmation.*

I went back to the living room where my mom was sitting. The room was quiet. She turned towards me and said, "Sharon, for some reason, I feel that you were just healed of bipolar disorder."

That healing left me a new woman. I remember waking up the next morning, amazed at how peaceful I felt. For the first time, my thoughts weren't racing and I didn't have to convince myself to get out of bed. I quit taking my medications, and I had no bad side effects from quitting the medicine. I stayed balanced in my reactions to life. Thank God.

But now I was in a new crisis. In my personal confusion, I hadn't noticed that my marriage was falling apart. My husband, Ivan, was gone longer hours than ever with his sales job. He seemed to barely tolerate me these days.

Now that I was healed, I could feel the cutting remarks and disparaging comments. Now, he said he was leaving me. I didn't really believe him until he packed up and moved in with a friend.

How had we gotten here? Thirteen years of marriage. Four children. We had to make it work. I had promised myself. I still remember standing in the middle of the road when I was eight years old, promising myself that my children would never go through divorce. They would have a loving home with two loving parents. Their family would be whole and peaceful and full of love. I'd never, ever, ever, ever, ever get divorced. But here we were.

I prayed and fasted that Ivan would agree to go to counseling with me. I was so hopeful that counseling would fix everything. My Christian counselor told me that I could take the heat more than Ivan could because of my relationship with Jesus. So every single appointment my husband criticized me, and I just sat there and took it. I was willing to do anything because I wanted my family back desperately. I didn't like being separated. I definitely didn't want to get divorced.

Then the final blow. Ivan recalled my having been diagnosed with bipolar disorder. He decided to blame me and my mental illness for his own horrible decisions. I told my counselor that Jesus had healed me. I had been symptom free for years.

My counselor couldn't get anywhere with my husband, so she decided I should agree to be retested—to put this to rest once and for all. I said I would do whatever it took. Ivan said I had to go to the very psychiatrist who had originally diagnosed me.

My family said I shouldn't get retested. They said that I would be risking losing custody of the children. Ivan could use my diagnosis against me. I felt so weak. I went into my prayer closet and saw the road less traveled. A giant was standing before me holding generations in bondage with his chains of fear. I saw Jesus—all powerful and ready to intercede. By His grace in that moment, courage soared in my heart. If my God had healed me, then He had this all worked out, too.

I went to my doctor and told him what was happening. He shook his head and said, "You don't have to do this." But I insisted that I did. He called the behavioral health center to get an appointment scheduled for me.

When I got there for my appointment, the place was so dark. I felt like a common criminal being escorted to the bathroom by an officer who collected my urine sample. After a blood draw and a lot of questions, I left in tears. *God, this is so hard. How can I get through this?*

My next appointment was with the psychiatrist who had initially diagnosed me. Did I mention that she was a Buddhist? She had no reason to validate my claim that God had healed me.

Although God provided a loving friend to be there with me, I still felt sick to my stomach. I knew I had to do this, but even with her next to me, I still felt alone. Then I remembered God was with me; I could feel His presence. I just needed to concentrate on that.

The psychiatrist called me back to her office. I told her that I believed that Jesus had healed me. I told her all about stopping my medications, and how I had experienced zero side effects (virtually unheard of with SSRI's). She said, "I'm writing your words,

'Jesus healed me,' but understand that these are not my words. I'm just transcribing what you are saying."

I knew she thought I was completely nuts! She continued to test me. I answered all her questions. I told her how for the last year I'd been juggling single parenthood, my new job, a son with Down Syndrome with his related therapies, and a toddler who had just learned to walk. To top things off, I was taking classes to learn how to maintain a budget. How could someone with bipolar disorder handle all of that stress un-medicated?

My psychiatrist said, "I can't explain it. Clearly you had bipolar disorder—see your chart? It's clear. It doesn't just go away. In 99% of cases, it's a lifetime disorder. You must be part of that 1%. I don't know how or why, but you definitely don't have bipolar disorder anymore or mental illness of any kind. And, yes, I will put that in writing for you."

She may not have known why, or how, but I did. Five years later, I still know Who healed me and Who restored my life. Ivan and I still ended up getting divorced, because it takes two to maintain a marriage. However, I got primary custody of my four children.

God not only healed me of a dysfunctional past, but he also kept me strong enough to create a stable future for my children. I'm so thankful that our past doesn't decide our future! God does.

Dear Maggie,

Wow. This is a hard letter to write. I've been thinking about what to say to you for years. Now that I know that you've been given three months to live, I suddenly realize that I have to write this now.

I FORGIVE YOU!

I really do. This has been a tough road for me. I've wanted to hurt you, lash out in anger, wish the worst on you. Luckily, I've had seven years to process and let God deal with me since James told me about the two of you.

My best friend and my husband betraying me for years without my knowing it···. It's hard to imagine anything hurting worse. "Till death do us part" and "we're closer than sisters" both hating me that much? Yeah, that's how it felt. Like you must have hated me that much.

Of course, now that I've lived on the other side of my divorce and James's marrying you, I understand that neither of you hated me. You were just selfish and desperate to find your own happiness.

Hurt people damage others because they are acting out from their own dark place. I know that I've unknowingly hurt people in the process of dealing with my pain. I didn't mean to, but I was blinded by my feelings and couldn't even consider the damage I might be causing anyone else.

I remember you telling me how you felt about your husband cheating on you. You just couldn't figure out what you had done wrong or what was so much better about her. You'd been married for 20 years when he left you for her. It seemed like she must be more valuable than you, because he chose her over you and your kids.

Did that make you feel like you would be worth more if you were the "other woman"? If someone chose you above their childhood sweetheart? Despite our being each other's first loves, James did choose you over me. Did that fix the betrayal from your husband?

Being rejected by the person we thought loved us unconditionally is devastating. To prove I was worth something, I wanted validation from a man. I NEEDED to be given attention, compliments, gifts. I wasn't okay alone.

One day, I realized why that "desperate divorcee" stereotype was so true. I was desperate to feel like I was worth loving. Honestly, with all the attention men will give to get sex, it's easy to confuse lust with love. To pretend that they actually care. That they mean all those wonderful compliments.

It's easy to stop thinking rationally and believe the lies. I actually bought into the "I've waited for you all my life" crap. "You're the most amazing lady I've ever met" made me feel like I must actually be worth something.

By the way, thank you for walking the road of being betrayed and rejected in front of me. I've made very different choices than I might have because I saw how unhappy you were with the results of your choices. From your example, I knew it wouldn't make me feel any better. I also knew that I wouldn't want to cause "the wife" the level

of pain I'd experienced. There was no one on earth
I hated THAT much.

It's crazy though, how hard it was to be thinking
about that when my "McDreamy" was romancing
me after the divorce. I just wanted to pretend
that he wasn't married. I wanted to believe that I
was that special, that he really loved me.

We started out as business friends. I never met his
wife, so it was easy to pretend she didn't exist.
We just had so much fun together. We could talk
about anything. Then there was the chemistry. He
was so handsome! It was harmless to be friends,
right? We cooked up all kinds of excuses to spend
time together.

I didn't wake up and realize that I, too, was
becoming the "other woman" until I let him kiss
me. It took every ounce of willpower I'd ever had
to break that off before it went any further. I
thank God that He helped me stop before I had to
deal with the guilt of breaking up another family.

Back to forgiving you. I remember telling you that
I forgave you when I was still married to James
and thought we were fixing things. You told me
you were sorry on that phone call. I thought
talking to you would give me closure. That

forgiving you, or at least saying I was forgiving you, would help me fix my marriage.

I guess it did make it last another couple of years. But you're married to him now, so it definitely wasn't the "magic pill" for keeping what I wanted. Forgiving you did get me out of the quicksand that wanted to suck me under right then.

I remember the night after I found out that you and James had been having an affair for years. I was awake that entire night in absolute torment. I'd had my sisters tell me that they thought something was going on between the two of you. My answer was that I trusted both of you. That even if you were locked in a room together, naked, that you would never do anything like that to me. That your love for me and for God, would stop you. Obviously, that was very naïve of me.

I've been in a lot of physical pain at different times over the years. From kidney stones and cyst ruptures to natural childbirth, I know what a 10 is on the pain scale. This emotional pain was a million times worse. I wanted to give in to the quicksand and disappear from life.

I cried until I was dehydrated. When I looked in the mirror, my face was so swollen that I looked like I'd had my wisdom teeth pulled again. I really wanted the "light at the end of the tunnel" to be an oncoming train!

James told me that y'all had broken up. That he had to tell me about the affair because he wanted to fix our marriage. The funny thing was that, when he confessed this, I thought our marriage was the best it had ever been.

We had a "surprise" baby to prove it! I know he had a hard time explaining that to you. You thought we were just housemates who were staying together for the kids' sake. You knew me well enough to know it had to be his baby despite his excuses that I must have been having an affair. Besides, she looks just like her older sister.

So, we went to a five star resort for a "second honeymoon" to fix our marriage. At the end of that week, I was sure we were closer than ever and could survive anything.

But, he left me for you a few months later. I filed for divorce. Then when y'all broke up, I took him back and filed a dismissal. I'd married him for "better or worse." This was just much "worse" than I'd ever expected. But God can heal anything, right? This time, when we said our vows during our second wedding on the beach, we promised each other and the kids that we would put God first and each other second.

I pulled out all the stops to be the wife that James would never want to leave. All I asked was for him to respect me enough to leave me before being with anyone else. I also told him that he couldn't communicate with you at all. I knew y'all had a codependent relationship. Any contact would lead to an affair again.

I told him that if he ever played that game again, I was done. Three strikes and you're out. Our marriage would be over. He'd lose everything.

Five years ago, I followed through on that promise. You won. He couldn't stay away from you, and I wasn't willing to share. I told him that he was going to hurt whoever he was with. I'd done my time; it was someone else's turn. Anger fueled me through the divorce process, but when it was all done, I was spent and alone. All I could think about

was how you had both betrayed me. I wanted you
both to pay for the pain you caused me and my
kids.

Then, I started realizing that my girls were better
off with your being the woman in James's life.
They'd known you most of their lives. I knew you
would take great care of them like you had when
you were my best friend. You helped me so much
during those years when I was so sick. I guess in
some ways, I abdicated my position as wife and
mother during that time. You filled that place
while James filled the void in your boys' life after
their dad bailed.

It took me a long time to realize that my
"codependent" relationship with you had invited
you into my marriage. It hurts me to admit that I
played a role in how things ended up. I made you a
part of my family without restriction. I didn't
mean for things to turn out the way they did, but
I did nothing to protect my husband or you from
the level of intimacy you developed while I was
constantly sick.

I didn't understand boundaries. I loved you both and
wanted you to be happy. I'm sorry that this made
you both susceptible to temptation.

Back to forgiving. I yelled at God that no human on earth could forgive this level of betrayal from the two people they trusted the most. But I couldn't get the Sermon on the Mount out of my head. "But I say unto you, love your enemies, bless them that curse you, do good to them that hate you, and pray for them which despitefully use you..." Matthew 5:44 And then of course: "For if ye forgive men their trespasses, your heavenly Father will also forgive you: But if ye forgive not men their trespasses, neither will your Father forgive your trespasses." Matthew 6:14,15.

I didn't really have a choice, did I? I definitely needed His forgiveness for my sins. I told God that I was definitely not capable of forgiving the two of you for this type of betrayal. He reminded me to "love," "bless," "do good," and "pray." That these would make the "forgive" a reality.

My emotions certainly didn't want to cooperate! So, I decided to obey God--despite how I felt. Every time I felt hatred, I spoke a blessing on both of you. Every time I thought of what you'd stolen from me, I tried to "do good" to you. My kids and I started praying for you both at bedtime.

Don't get me wrong, this was the hardest, most painful process I've ever chosen. Like the chemo and radiation you've experienced, I thought the "cure" for my hatred would kill me. But it hasn't killed me. It has freed me.

God has healed my body and my soul. I'm more at peace and happier than I've ever been in my life. I'm the healthiest person I know. I clearly remember the pain, but it doesn't have the power to hurt me now. I would never have chosen this path to healing and wholeness, but I wouldn't trade it for the world.

I hope you will be restored and completely healed. I know God can heal you of cancer. He's healed people in my own family. Please forgive me and anyone else in your life who's hurt or betrayed you. We were best friends, so I know that your list of hurt and betrayal is a really long one. I also know it's possible, with God's help, to really forgive. I want you to have the peace and joy that comes from releasing the hatred and hurt.

I know this letter seems crazy, but if I've learned anything through this process, it's that there's freedom and healing in forgiving. God keeps reminding me that you and James are still my

"brother and sister in Christ."
You are the other parents that my children have
to look to for love and validation. I've realized
that the best thing for my kids is to have all of
us be healthy, loving parents to them. We all need
to love them and put God first.

This letter is much longer than I planned, but I
hope it makes sense.

Blessings,
Lavender

To appoint unto them that mourn in Zion, to give unto them beauty for ashes, the oil of joy for mourning, the garment of praise for the spirit of heaviness; that they might be called trees of righteousness, the planting of the Lord, that he might be glorified.

Isaiah 61:3

Dear Me,

I saw you. Lying in a heap on the empty floor, heartbroken and shattered. Oh, how I wish I could have told you then, that it really was going to be alright. The weight on your shoulders...it wasn't for you to carry. God would carry it for you, if you would let Him.

I'm so proud of you now. You've had quite a few victories. I love how you put your children first when Darryl left you with your house in foreclosure. You told them it was going to be an adventure.

God was moving you all soon. You were not sure when or where, but He was giving you an adventure. They were traumatized when their dad left, but not when they left their home. Their eyes were looking ahead—so excited about the adventure you had described.

What about the time you walked across the backyard at dusk, after a long day? You were unable to think one more thought; unable to do one more thing; unable to force one more smile. They were inside, with dirty diapers and fragile hearts, waiting for you.

Your victory was in reaching out to Him. You didn't trust much back then, but you mustered what you had and pleaded towards Heaven. *Jesus, please, intercede for me. I can't do it. I can't make it. I can't do this anymore. It's too much to carry.*

Do you remember? You do. You can still feel the peace that swept over your heart in that instance. You remember walking inside and laughing with those precious little ones. They had no idea you were aching inside because He provided such an elaborate miracle in that moment. He gave you what you needed, to be just what they needed.

All these victories hold the common thread of help coming from our Lord God. He became your lifeline, and you began to trust Him. Oh how I wish you had trusted Him more and sooner. Yes, the load was too much, but you learned. With His help, it was much lighter.

You made it after all.

Love,
Ivy

I Hated My Own Son

I hear my son Wade ask me where his socks are, but I don't turn to answer. I can't stand the sight of him. I want to kill him! I don't want him to see the hate on my face, so I keep my back to him as I tell him to check the laundry basket that's overflowing with clean socks, underwear and t-shirts.

I feel guilty for my feelings, but I don't know how to change them. He's only thirteen, but when I look at him, all I can see is a monster. What happened to my baby boy? What happened to my feelings of unconditional love?

We're finally ready to drive to court where a judge will decide what happens next. I'm torn between wanting the judge to throw the book at Wade and wanting to protect him from the choices he's made. I'm developing a migraine from the war inside my head. The medicine I took isn't helping at all. This nightmare caught me completely off guard.

It started a few weeks ago, when two policemen showed up at my door. I innocently asked them if I could help them. They showed me their badges. They said they needed to talk to me privately, without the kids. I sent the boys outside and asked the officers what was wrong. They asked me to sit down.

Uh oh, this was going to be bad. The looks on their faces scared me. Why were they feeling sorry for me? I sat down with a growing feeling of dread.

"Where is Wade?" they asked. "At a friend's house. Why? What did he do wrong? Did he steal something? I'm always telling him that doing stupid stuff will get you in trouble! Or did he hit someone? Was he smoking, or drinking, or at a party that got out of control?" I was babbling. I was afraid. I started crying.

"No, ma'am. We need to ask you some questions first. Then we'll tell you what is going on. Here's some tissue. Please stop crying," the older one said. The younger one looked really uncomfortable.

I managed to pull myself together a little. I wished my husband were here. He's not the boys' dad, but he loves them as if he were. As I found out what was going on, I got more and more sick to my stomach. I finally ran to the bathroom, sure I was going to throw up.

They were accusing my son of molesting his stepsister. She told her real dad that Wade was sneaking into her room at night and touching her. She claimed that it had been going on for over a year! She had to be lying! If not, I was going to kill him. I looked in the bathroom mirror. I saw my face as a young girl who'd just thrown up after the same thing had happened to me.

I had been molested off and on for two years by that college boy I couldn't seem to get away from. I would think he was away at college, and then I'd feel hands covering my mouth as his strong arms pulled me into a dark shed. He'd never raped me, but his touching me made me feel so dirty!

I was eleven when it started happening and couldn't figure out what was going on. I couldn't understand how my body could feel good when he touched me, but my mind screamed "RUN! He's hurting you!" If I knew he was home from college, I would hide or make sure I was in a large group whenever I was outside.

I couldn't tell anyone because he said he'd tell them that I was "asking for it." I lived a very sheltered life and had no idea what I was asking for. I just knew it was bad and I'd get in trouble.

Now, I was looking at myself in the mirror as the mother of my own worst nightmare! I splashed water on my face and faced the police again. I felt like I was in a trance. The rest of the last two weeks have been a blur. Wade admitted that he'd undressed her and touched her, but he was adamant that he had not "hurt" her. I found out he'd been looking at pornography since a friend had introduced him to it.

When we get to court, the judge follows the recommendations of the psychologist and social workers. Consequences, but no jail. His step sisters will be kept away from any contact with him.

Counseling, community service, and probation style restrictions should help him get back on track. I am relieved.

I know that he is just a hormonal boy from a broken family who's acting out. I know he saw his stepmother naked after he found out that his dad's affair with her had led to our divorce. I know that he is hurting and confused and doesn't understand the consequences of his choices. I know that he is just a lost boy and not a hardened predator (confirmed by the psychologist), but I can't separate myself from the little girl I had been when I was molested. I can't look at him without reliving the hurt and shame I had felt.

How am I ever going to be the mother he needs to help him change directions from the path he is on? I know I have to start dealing with my own pain and damage. I call my best friend, Barb. I spill my guts and all my dirty laundry. She's the only person I know who won't look down on me. The fear, shame, pain, anger, and confusion are overwhelming.

She tells me about a part of her story that is very similar, but that she's never told me before. I didn't know that her son had gotten into trouble for touching other kids at school and on the playground.

"I had to forgive myself, the guy who hurt me as a child, and my ex-husband. He had set such a bad example with his affair. Like David's sin with Bathsheba, adultery opens doors to consequences. Remember King David's son raped his own sister after David's sin? Well, I've prayed against generational curses that can be passed down in families. God can forgive and stop the patterns of damage."

She continued, "My son hasn't shown any signs of that behavior for five years. I've even had to forgive my son for hurting me with his behavior. God helped me get past my own struggle with hating my son. I'm so sorry you're having to go through this, too! You can do this. God will help you. Love you, girl!"

What she said makes sense. Maybe I can survive the shame and fear. Maybe I can feel love for my son again. I realize that God can bring healing, not only for me, but for him, too.

This is horribly ugly and dark, but if it stops him from continuing on this path, it will be worth it. According to the doctor, he's getting help early enough to prevent the pattern from continuing. He's very remorseful and repentant.

God, thank you that this came to light in time to get us both help. Please help me to be the mom he needs to help him get completely free from pornography. Help him become a protector of women, not an abuser. Thank you that we can deal with this psychological cancer in the early stages. We have hope for full healing. This mess will NOT continue to grow in the dark until it's destroyed him completely. Help me love my son unconditionally with Your love. Thank you, Father.

Fear thou not; for I am with thee: be not dismayed; for I am thy God: I will strengthen thee; yea, I will help thee; yea, I will uphold thee with the right hand of my righteousness.

Isaiah 41:10

Submit!

By Rue

I heard a car door close. I started to panic. My heart was racing. Alvarez, my husband who demanded to be called "Al," was home early. What had I forgotten to do? The house was spotless. Supper was almost ready.

I couldn't think of anything, but that didn't mean I wasn't going to get in trouble. When Al walked in the door I was trying to help my son with his homework while the rice finished cooking.

"Maria, what are you doing?" Al demanded as he walked in the door. When I didn't answer, he barked, "Go out on the porch and wait for me." My heart sank. Not again! I must be doing something very wrong. But what? In the end it didn't really matter. Even when I did exactly what my husband told me to do, something was always wrong.

When he came out, Al started yelling at me for helping our son with his homework. He told me that I was never to help any of the children with their homework. In fact, I was never to spend any time with any of our five children. How had we come to this?

Once I had asked Jesus into my life, I wanted to serve Him with all my heart. I wanted to be involved in the church in any way that I could. Al and I met a pastor who seemed to be passionate about God. We joined his church and helped with every service and outreach the pastor was leading. Even when the pastor preached in other churches, we went with him. We never missed a service.

"Submit!!" The word pounded at me from the pulpit week after week. The pastor would expound upon every scripture that had anything to do with the subject of submission. I looked up all of the scripture references and then tried to follow them.

Al seemed to revel in the "submission" teachings. However, there were times when obeying my husband's commands seemed to be wrong to me. But God's word was telling me to obey him, right? Every Bible study and every lesson our pastor preached seemed to be about submission! I thought, *God, you must be talking to me.* I was trying so hard to obey God...

Things between my husband and me got progressively worse. Al started accusing me of being a "Jezebel." In the Bible, Jezebel was a wicked queen who would stop at nothing to get her own way. She was controlling and connected to witchcraft. The prophets foretold the gruesome death she would suffer on account of her many sins.

Al said that, if I didn't do what he wanted, I would be responsible for drawing God's wrath down on me and our children. I lived in constant fear--fear of making the wrong move, fear of losing my children, fear of somehow causing their deaths.

By this time, verbal abuse was a part of my daily life. At the dinner table each night, with the children present, Al judged me for being a controlling woman and not obeying simple commands. I was accused of disobedience and rebellion. No matter what I did, no matter how hard I tried, I was told that I had somehow "sinned."

The time came when Al forbade me to have any contact with my own children. I could not drive them anywhere. I could not to go to their ball games or school activities. I couldn't even kiss them goodnight. It was more than I could bear.

How could I break off all contact with them? I loved them more than life itself! I didn't want to be responsible for my punishment extending to them, so I did what my husband demanded. I was only allowed to be the housekeeper – and he expected everything to be done perfectly.

One day when I got home from work, I found a note saying that Al had taken the children on vacation. The note did not say where they had gone. I waited to hear something from them, but there was no communication. I heard nothing at all for ten, long days.

I worried and suffered alone in silence. Every year that he did this, I was shocked and devastated. There was never any warning, just an empty house and a note.

Eventually, Al kicked me out of our bedroom because of my "Jezebel" spirit. For months, I slept on a couch in a little room on the third floor. Each night, when everyone else was asleep, I would dance before the Lord. I would silently sing and raise my hands, while tears of rejection and anguish poured down my cheeks. I would pray, asking God to deliver me from this horrible spirit that was living in me.

I never felt delivered from "Jezebel," but I did experience God's presence. His "peace that passes understanding" would settle over me. Then I could rest.

One day, Al blatantly told me that God was going to kill me. He started kicking me out of the house with no money and locking me out until after the kids were asleep. Other times, he would send me on random errands that made no sense. He explained to me that he didn't want God to accidently kill my family if they were with me.

Apparently, God wasn't killing me quickly enough, so Al decided to lend a hand by putting me in risky situations. Al didn't believe in divorce, so my death would be his only escape from his marriage to such a "wicked woman."

I, on the other hand, felt that I had no escape. I didn't think I could tell anyone what was happening in my home without making things worse, so I kept silent. I couldn't abandon my children, so I stayed. By this point, Al had quit speaking directly to me. He would just criticize me to "his" children.

Since I was excluded from everything, I felt invisible. I lived each day with my soul locked up in solitary confinement. I was so torn between believing that a loving God would never want this and wondering if everyone at church could really be that wrong...

All along I knew that church was probably the best place to talk to other people, but I had been brainwashed to believe that I was the problem in my home. I didn't want to bring shame on my family because of my rebellion, so I kept quiet. That ended the day God's light shone through my darkness. God met me at church one Sunday and turned my life around.

A woman who was visiting the church sat next to me. After the service, she asked me one simple question: "You have such an amazing voice. Why don't you sing in the choir?" My answer, "My husband won't let me," opened the floodgates, and I couldn't quit crying.

She told me that she was a Christian counselor. She took me aside into an empty room where I told her my story. It was the first time that I had admitted my situation to anyone!

Tears streamed down her face as she said to me, "Maria, you are NOT the problem. This is not your fault! Your husband is the one with the problem. Al should be covering you with God's love. When your husband is abusing you instead of holding that loving umbrella over you, you no longer have to obey him. You are to submit to your husband 'as unto the Lord,' but only if your husband is loving you 'as Christ loved the church and gave Himself for it.'"

As she prayed for me, the entire room was filled with a cloud of white smoke. God's presence was tangible. I could feel it all around me. When she finished praying, I was free. Free from all of the fear. Free from all of the deception.

Joy flowed over me for the first time in years. I could see what had happened and how wrong it was. My home was under a spirit of control that was trying to destroy us, but I was not the source of the problem.

The next day, I went to an old friend who was a pastor in nearby Dallas. She sent me to a counselor, who sent me to a lawyer. The attorney and I spent a week strategizing how to get the kids and me out of this mess without anyone getting hurt.

Once the plan was in place, I picked up my children from school for the first time in a year. They were surprised, but happy when I told them we were going away for a few days. While we were gone, the police showed up with a court order and evicted my husband.

I did not want a divorce. I believed in keeping my vows "until death do us part," but the control and abuse were destroying our family. Al consistently refused to even try to change in any way, so I had to protect myself and our children. He never admitted to doing anything wrong. The amazing thing was that through the whole messy divorce process, God gave us peace.

Once I knew that our problems weren't my fault, I was full of joy! God loved me! He had never intended any of this to happen to me or to my children. He had never wanted me to be hurt, humiliated, or shamed. Jesus bore all of my sins on the cross so that I wouldn't have to suffer under their weight. He came to set me free. He had never left me.

Since the divorce, I have continued to heal from the abuse. God has ministered to me and my children through countless people who have shown us true Christian love and support. I now have primary custody of my children and get to do everything with them. I don't mind caring for the five of them on my own. I am just so grateful that I get to be a part of their lives.

My girls smile again and even laugh. My boys play games and tell ridiculous jokes. We've all quit looking over our shoulders to see if someone is judging what we're doing. We are enjoying our freedom, more than most, because we lived in a prison for so long.

God is no respecter of persons. What he did for me, He can do for you. Whatever your situation, your hurt, your shame, just call out to Him. Then wait with expectation. Your Savior is close at hand, and He WILL deliver you. Only He can turn your mourning into dancing again!

*But as it **is** written, Eye hath not seen, nor ear heard, neither have entered into the heart of man, the things which **God** hath prepared for them that **love** him.*

1 Corinthians 2:9

Inside **Out**

By Larkspur

The perfect family
On the outside
But personal punching bag
On the inside

Looking my best
On the outside
Bruised, suffocated, imprisoned
On the inside

Shown off to the world
On the outside
Isolated, punished, cursed
On the inside

Makeup, clothes, shoes, hair beautiful
On the outside
Fear, pain, doubt, insecurity hiding
On the inside

Professional Fashionista
On the outside
Ugly, torn and battered
On the inside

Talented and successful
On the outside
Nothing ever good enough
On the inside

Like cancer that doesn't show
On the outside
Eating away at my very life
On the inside

Man controlling
On the outside
Pleading for God's help
On the inside

Crying tears of brokenness
On the outside
Healing balm soothing me
On the inside

Rejected, discarded, unwanted
On the outside
Treasured
On the inside

Not caring what others think
On the outside
My savior loving me
On the inside

Darkness and storms may come
On the outside
But love, peace and joy abide
On the inside

Smiling, Loving, Sharing
On the outside
Redeeming life bubbling
On the inside

O give thanks unto the Lord; for he is good; for his mercy endureth for ever.

1 Chronicles 16:34

Don't Abandon the Ship!

By Yarrow

Call me a wimp. Call me a coward. Tell me that I still have some emotional issues that I need to work through. You would be right on all three counts. That doesn't change the fact that you are only going to get the middle of my story. I am leaving out the gory details from the first part of my marriage. Honestly, I am not ready to go back into that dark hole.

I am enjoying the sunshine, intermixed with a few cloudy days and an occasional storm. I am just not ready to dissect the hurricane that I left behind. When you are in a lifeboat, with a beautiful tropical island in sight, you don't start jumping around and messing with the equilibrium of your raft. If you've ever been in my shoes, you know exactly what I am talking about.

You see, my story is still a work in progress. God is in the process of painting a beautiful picture on my canvas, but it's not done yet. My husband and I still haven't ridden off into the sunset – but we have escaped the hurricane. I want to share with you some of the things that have brought us to where we are.

DeWayne and I got married hoping, as all couples do, that our marriage would be one of the good ones. I remember his telling me before we got married that he wanted an equal partnership between us. That sounded great to me. We would discuss things together and work out solutions that we both were happy with. Neither one of us would try to control the other or run the show. Yeah, right!

The honeymoon ended, and we moved to New Orleans. Then the problems started. In DeWayne's family, his mother ruled the roost. He despised his dad for being a spineless wimp who did whatever his mom wanted him to do. Desperately wanting to be nothing like his dad, DeWayne needed to be in control in our relationship.

When I use the word control, you need to understand that he had every intention of being the marionette master. I was supposed to dance depending on which strings he pulled. There were "emotion" strings, "affection" strings, "action" strings – so many strings. I was jerked around emotionally and sometimes physically, at his whim. That hurt a lot! The emotional abuse was painful and random. There was no way to escape by doing the right thing or saying the right thing. Nothing was logical or made any sense...

I prayed. We were both Christians. I prayed for God to fix DeWayne and for God to fix me, but mostly for God to fix him. Over time I started to become bitter and sarcastic. I understood why the archetype of the bitter housewife existed. I no longer thought that that woman was crazy. She probably used to be a nice, loving woman who had just been driven to the edge of insanity. Her bitter tongue was her way of surviving. I totally got it.

Then I began to feel the darkness build up inside. At one point I knew that if I didn't change something, I would develop cancer or have an emotional breakdown. I could feel where things were headed. The bitterness and the hurt were eating me up inside. Something had to change – and it didn't look like I was having much success changing DeWayne. So... that meant that I would have to change.

God began to show me that when it was time for me to stand before Him and give account for all of my actions, the "but, DeWayne," card would get me nowhere.

"God, I know that I yelled and screamed and got extremely angry. But DeWayne..." All God would want to know from me would be how I had responded. What had I done? DeWayne would have to answer to God for his own actions. Ouch! I was in trouble. My *Get Out of Jail Free* card had just been declared invalid.

So, with God's help, I began to focus on my actions and my reactions. In Matthew 5:44 Jesus tells us...

> *"Love your enemies, bless them that curse you, do good to them that hate you, and pray for them which despitefully use you, and persecute you..."*

Sometimes those words may describe those nearest and dearest to you. The change in me began as a decision to obey God. The feelings came later. Many times I would pray with my mouth for God to bless DeWayne. What I really wanted God to do was strike him down with lightning!

However, in time, God began to change my heart. He began to show me that many of the things that DeWayne did were a result of his own hurts and his own pain. He began to give me a compassionate heart and helped me separate my husband from his actions. The very sweet, thoughtful, kind man that I had married was still there - even if he did dress up as an ogre more often than I liked.

The problems were still there. The nightmare was not over, but my reality was different. I was changing. Anger and bitterness were losing their grip on me. I could feel healing happening inside.

In time, God began working on DeWayne, too. He began to make a real commitment to serve God. He went to several workshops and conferences that turned him around 180 degrees for a period of time. The first time it happened I was so happy! It was hard when he relapsed into his old ways. But, truth be told, I relapsed into my old ways sometimes, too. At times, it seemed that the ups and downs were taking us more downhill than up.

Things got to the point where I began to seriously question whether or not divorce was the right thing to do for our children. I didn't want them growing up scarred by our hurts. I didn't want this lifestyle to be their "normal." I felt like I was hanging over a cliff at the end of a frayed rope.

God! Help! What should I do? I wasn't exactly excited when He answered that question. He directed me to get my Bible. It opened to the story of Paul and the shipwreck on the island of Melita. He clearly spoke to me through the following verses:

> *"Then fearing lest we should have fallen upon rocks, they cast four anchors out of the stern, and wished for the day. And as the shipmen were about to flee out of the ship..... Paul said to the centurion and to the soldiers, **Except these abide in the ship, ye cannot be saved**."*
> (Acts 27: 29–31)

Clear as a bell I KNEW that leaving my marriage at that time would not save me and my children. It would bring us harm. The warning was stern, but very clear to me. So we hung on tightly to ride out the storm.

God helped me to stand up to my husband and to no longer live in fear. I came to realize, that no matter what I did, I could not stop DeWayne from having bad days. I could not keep him from getting angry and yelling at me. I began to see that his words did not have to define who I was. I began to see that arguing with DeWayne did not help him "see the light." He had no idea how many times I bit my tongue and did not respond, because of how many times I lost the battle and yelled back!

But, the tide was changing. God was strengthening me, maturing me, and healing me. As

God spoke to me and I obeyed, He was free to answer my prayers and begin healing my marriage.

I can't pinpoint the exact day or moment when it happened, but God gave me a new husband. He transformed my husband's life to the point where other people began to notice a change in him, too. God opened DeWayne's eyes, and he began to see clearly how he had behaved in the past. God began to heal him, too. The change has been real. We still have some clouds and an occasional storm, but our lives have changed. I am looking forward to the next chapter in our story.

Through the storms, God showed me the importance of focusing on the areas where I need to change. God showed me the importance of obedience to Him. He showed me that He is a God of miracles. Now, I can enjoy the journey, because the ending to our story is in His hands.

Rock Bottom

By Tansy

Rock bottom. This is what it feels like. I felt like every part of my being had been shattered. I'd been in a dark hole forever, it seemed, but this was different. I couldn't move or breathe or think. Agony. Pure, unadulterated, emotional agony! Physical pain would be an improvement.

This is why people end it all! Death would have to be so much better than this, I thought. *Besides, my heart and soul have just been murdered. Why not my body? Actually, why couldn't they have killed me? Anything but this....*

It all started with an invitation to dinner by old friends. Peter and Denise Jones were pastors from our church in Arizona. They had been foster parents to my husband, Pierre, when he was a teenager, so we both looked up to them as parents and mentors. Since we'd gotten married and moved to Pennsylvania ten years ago, we had only seen them a couple of times.

This would be a real treat. We met at a nice restaurant, ready to have a relaxing meal after an exhausting day at work. The twins were with their aunt, so we didn't have to worry about them. I took a deep breath and focused on the menu.

We ordered our meals as we caught up on all the changes in their family and ours. We were finishing our food when the discussion got a little more serious. They told us how two of their daughters had been going through a tough time.

They had recently seen all nine of their children at a family reunion in Texas. We knew their whole family, so we were interested to know what was wrong. I should have known that something wasn't quite right with this whole meeting, but I was so relieved to get a break from the twins and work that I was just enjoying a meal out.

Denise started explaining how they had found out that Shannon and Terri had been molested as girls. Evidently, this had messed them up enough to explain their choices after they left home. They were both happily married, but they had evidently acted out a bit before settling down.

Denise explained how shocked she was that Shannon had never told her what was going on. Terri had always kept secrets, so that was no surprise. But why wouldn't a daughter ask her mother, or even father, for help?

I interrupted her to tell her my story. I knew why they had never told anyone. Growing up in a small church, I had never told anyone my story, either. I explained to them how I had blamed myself for the sexual abuse I'd experienced when I was little. A man in my church had raped me. He told me it was my fault and that everyone would hate me if they found out. I started crying as I told her that I completely understood where her girls were coming from.

"When you are violated in that way, you don't think you are worth loving. You see yourself as damaged goods, especially in an old fashioned church like ours. You knew the rules, and you knew the consequences for breaking them. I'm sure Shannon and Terri had to grow up enough to realize it wasn't their fault, before they could tell you."

I told them that I had waited until I was much older before admitting anything to my parents. I knew they loved me, but I was still afraid of losing that love.

What Peter said next catapulted me into this black hole that seemed to be filled with razor blades. He looked at my husband and said, "Pierre, we've always thought of you as a son. How on earth could you do that to my little girls? We trusted you. They were your sisters for you to protect. How could you hurt them? You may not have raped them, but touching them inappropriately caused real emotional damage."

As my soul was being sliced to shreds, I heard Denise ask my husband to apologize to her daughters. My body sat there and listened to them accuse him of abusing their trust. They expected him to treat their girls like biological sisters. This made me feel like I was a little girl again. Only this time, there was more than one person torturing me. I couldn't separate what they were saying from what I'd lived through as a child.

Peter and Denise said they forgave Pierre but wanted him to write letters to their girls explaining that he was sorry for hurting them. Peter warned Pierre that Terri's husband had wanted to kill him when he found out. Evidently, we were lucky that we lived so far away.

All I could think about was wanting to die. Now. Before I had to listen to another word. Finally, everyone stood up and said goodbye. The Joneses gave me hugs and said they appreciated our meeting them.

I had no idea how to respond. I ran to the car in a panic to get away from the last couple of hours. Then the panic got worse. My worst nightmare was getting in the car with me!

I always ran into Pierre's arms when something was hurting me. He was my protector, my strength. But now, I needed protection from him. My brain told me that he was my husband, not my rapist, but my soul was shrieking for help! I couldn't move, couldn't open my mouth to scream. This must all be a nightmare.

Wake up! Wake up! I yelled in my head. *Make this nightmare stop!*

But I was locked in a car with my rapist! Why couldn't someone have killed me before this? Or killed him. I didn't care who died. I just knew I couldn't survive the pain of living. Not for even one more second. But I didn't die and neither did Pierre. I finally realized that he was telling me that he was sorry. He explained that he'd never meant to hurt the girls.

Pierre told me about how he hadn't understood proper boundaries when he was growing up. He'd had a female babysitter molest him when he was little and didn't realize it was that big of a deal. He said he'd touched the Jones girls out of curiosity when he'd had the opportunity, but had never caused them any pain. He was very definite about not having hurt anyone.

Though no one explained proper boundaries to him, he'd stopped because it made him feel bad. He promised that he'd never touched another girl like that since he'd turned fourteen. He just wished someone had explained private boundaries to him as a child after he'd been molested. If he had understood, he would never have touched anyone.

I started crying. Fear, pain, rage, pain, shame, pain—it all hurt too much. Pierre ushered me into the house and to our room so that his sister, who was babysitting, wouldn't see me and ask what was wrong. I was like a rag doll. After he made sure the twins were okay and his sister had left, he came back to our room.

The torment in my mind was so bad, that what I saw was a rapist walk into my room. I wanted to scream and hide. Instead, I closed my eyes and remembered that Pierre was my husband. I was so torn between seeing him as my shelter and seeing him as a monster.

Pierre was the one who had helped me work past the damage from my childhood. He was the first man I had felt I could trust. He had slowly helped me open up and trust again. I had committed to forever with him. "Until death do us part" was in our vows before God. Now, I wanted the "death do us part."

Somehow, I had to escape myself. Suicide wasn't an option because God said it was murder. I turned toward the TV. I looked for the worst psycho serial killer show I could find. Over the next week, I watched twenty hours a day of twisted, abusive, murderous, painful shows. In these shows, the damage was worse than mine, right? And, they caught the bad guy at the end.

I refused to see anyone except Pierre. Like a victim of Stockholm Syndrome, I needed him to help me deal with the damage he was causing me. He would hold me while I sobbed.

I told him that he'd better get me professional help or he'd lose me permanently. I wasn't sure if I'd actually get up the courage to kill myself or if I'd just slide into a psychotic state of some sort. I just knew I couldn't survive this for very long. It was all in my head, but I couldn't stop the torment.

I couldn't deal with seeing my best friend and lifetime partner as my abuser. What if he'd hurt other girls? What if he was a true pedophile and not just a curious boy with no boundaries? He definitely preferred I keep myself shaved completely smooth like a little girl. But didn't most modern guys like a "clean playground"? The torment wasn't letting up at all.

Finally, he told me he'd found a Christian ministry in Missouri that specialized in healing. They had a good reputation for helping people get rid of different types of psychoses. He had booked me for a week long seminar that would include individualized ministry. If I needed more, I could choose to stay for a second week.

In my nightmare, I'd kept a running conversation with God. So when Pierre told me about the week of treatment, I asked God if He was going to help me. The answer to my question came in the form of a picture in my head.

I pictured a surgical suite like on the TV shows I was watching. Three really bright lights were shining down on me. I was spread eagled on the table. God was the surgeon and was telling me that I would have "open life" surgery. If I would let Him, God would remove sickness, damage, and disease. I was desperate enough to agree to anything if it would stop the tormenting pain.

The week I went for help, a lot of my preconceived ideas about God, religion and the Bible were flipped upside down. I knew I couldn't keep my prior perspectives because those hadn't been able to help me. I needed something that would change my life. So, I listened and participated with an open mind. As the week progressed, I cried a lot but felt like everything was getting lighter.

Through the teachings, I learned that I could be healed physically and emotionally. Spiritual and emotional damage had affected me physically. That was crazy. I was sick so much. If it was viral, I was always the first to catch it. Then, there was the laundry list of allergies, thyroid problems, digestive issues. The back problems from multiple accidents kept me in constant pain. The migraines and depression kept me medicated. The list was really long.

Then there was the issue of my female system. I had experienced nothing but pain from being female. From a dozen cysts rupturing, to vulvar vestibulitis and debilitating periods, everything was messed up. According to my doctor, it was a miracle I'd had the twins. I just knew that I had always hated being a woman. Could I really get healed of all that? Six months before, I'd started verbally choosing life and thanking God for making me a woman (that was tough). Now, I started seeing that God **could** actually heal me.

If I repented and separated myself from the damaging influences, I could be healed of the physical damage. I actively participated in the process at this seminar because I didn't want to miss out on anything God might do for me.

By the end of the week, I was a different person. I felt so connected to God. I was no longer in constant torment and emotional pain. My back didn't hurt. I was eating the foods I was allergic to. I had quit all my medications, and yet I felt the best I had in years. Wow. God had really done a lot of surgery.

On my last day there, a couple I talked to for a few minutes said that I was obviously just one of those "naturally happy" people. I laughed. Happy had never been used to describe me. Smart, serious, hardworking, kind, and generous might be used, but never happy. What a difference one week had made in my life.

I went home a completely different person. When I saw Pierre this time, I saw him as the man I'd fallen in love with. I forgave him for his mistakes as a teenager. Christ had died for him, too. I was ready to see how my healing would make our marriage better.

The physical healing made sex enjoyable for the first time in my life. I no longer had to get drunk to be able to deal with the physical pain that had been caused by the vulvar vestibulitis. Without the expensive surgery the specialist had recommended, I was healed. I actually wanted intimacy. We could finally have a real "honeymoon"!

Don't get me wrong, I still had to fight the victim thoughts. I still had to reject the fear of Pierre being a pedophile. The difference was that now I could fight it. I wasn't stuck in torment. The thoughts would attack me less often. I could stay married to Pierre and honor my vows without feeling suicidal.

Then, we went to stay at a friend's house in Virginia. She had an eight year old daughter. I panicked. I was a little girl bringing an abuser into her house. I couldn't stay there and risk her getting molested. All the fear and pain hit me again. Crying, I told Pierre we couldn't stay there. The panic made it hard to catch my breath, so we made some lame excuse and left.

I thought I was free from all that. I didn't realize situations could trigger everything again. I went back through my training. I used the tools I had been given to deal with the panic. Several hours of prayer later, I was at peace again. I apologized to Pierre for my reaction. He said that he knew I was doing my best, but he wished we could just go back to the way things were before the Joneses showed up.

Over the next few months, I asked God to give me a prayer partner who could help me with the process of dealing with these types of situations. Pierre would get so mad and hurt when I'd start panicking about him possibly being a pedophile. I couldn't tell anyone else. They'd hate me for bringing someone like that into their lives. I especially couldn't tell my own family. They might reject me just like the entire Jones clan had.

One day in church, I felt God prompt me to talk to one of the prayer warriors. Miss Betty Ann was known for being a woman of God whose prayers got answered. I couldn't tell her about my nightmare! But the feeling wouldn't leave, so I asked to talk to her privately. She smiled and agreed.

I had to fight the panic as I started telling Miss Betty Ann about needing prayer support to deal with a very ugly situation. She listened as I cried and blubbered through my story about the Joneses showing up. I explained about getting raped and the nightmarish fear that my husband was a pedophile. She started laughing. What? I'd expected a horrified reaction, not laughter.

She then explained that she was laughing at God's perfect wisdom. She knew why God had directed me to talk to her. Only God knew she was uniquely equipped to pray with me about this. Then she told me how her ex-husband had actually molested two of her nieces while she was married to him. They had quit visiting her at home but hadn't told her why until after her divorce. She knew what it actually felt like to have brought the perp into her family. She explained that her family had forgiven her.

She believed my fears were due to my own childhood trauma and were not an actual problem with my husband. Either way, I would survive. She knew that God would help me. She prayed with me. She also said she would keep praying for me.

I kept giving everything to God. Over time, I got stronger and the panic attacks got further apart. I knew I could survive because I'd had someone else tell me they had survived. Miss Betty Ann was a beautiful expression of God redeeming a bad situation. If she could become who she was, there was hope for me.

I hated that I had to go through this situation, but I knew that I wouldn't trade it for all the healing I had gotten as a result. I was healthy and felt good most of the time. My back was healed, so I wasn't in constant pain.

"Rock bottom" had just about taken me out, but God had used it to bring healing and restoration in so many areas of my life. What Satan had meant for evil, God had used for good.

*But **God**, who **is** rich in mercy, for his great **love**
wherewith he **loved** us,*

Ephesians 2:4

Life Preserver

By Violet

Sinking to the bottom
Nowhere to turn
No way to breathe
As the waves pound
Lost in the vast ocean of life
Massive tidal waves
Crashing down on my little boat

In the middle of a hurricane
There is no light
Shining down on my turbulent waters
Wind blasting and waves bashing
The life right out of me
The boat gone, but the life ring
Stuck around my waist keeping me alive

Battered and bruised to exhaustion
Yet a prisoner of hope
I close my eyes to the storm
Clinging to the ring encircling me
Everything I loved invisible
In the destruction
Dreams shattered and destroyed

No land in sight
Nothing to reach for in the darkness
Complete isolation
Nothing but pain, fear and turmoil
pushing me under
Wind's fury beating torrents of rain
Trying to drown me

Nothing but a little ring around my soul
When out of nowhere
A destroyer mows me down
Shoving me into the blackest depths
No one can survive this weight
It's over this time

Why art thou cast down, oh my soul?
Why art thou disquieted within me?
Trust thou in God!
God is my salvation
My present help in time of trouble
If He is for me,
Who can be against me?

The life preserver holds me tight
As I fight my way out
from under the crushing hulk
Struggling to rise
Towards hope and life
Reaching the surface to breathe once more
With God as my Life Preserver
I know NOTHING can ever keep me down!

For his merciful kindness is great toward us: and the truth of the Lord endureth for ever. Praise ye the Lord.

Psalm 117:2

Food Addict

By Lilac

I stood on the scales and realized that I had gained 72 pounds in 6 months! Where there used to be bones or muscles visible, it was all round and smooth. I was NOT pregnant. I was not on medication. I did not have a disease. I was just addicted to food. This was a first for me, and I had no idea what to do about it.

I remembered seeing overweight people eating huge plates of food and thinking, *Just quit eating so much! You wouldn't be that big if you just didn't eat so much.* Since I'd become addicted, I had a completely different perspective. I understood the struggle to fight overeating food when that was all I could think about. My stomach never felt full, even when it hurt from eating too much. The horrible feeling of something pulling me to the kitchen...

It all started when my boyfriend broke up with me. I thought he was the love of my life. I had just moved all the way across the country to be close to him, when he dumped me. He told me that he'd only wanted me because he couldn't have me. Once he knew that I cared and was ready for a serious relationship, he was no longer interested in me. I was absolutely devastated and started filling that void with food.

When I realized I was getting fat, I tried crash diets. I did well on the ones that included no food because I would avoid all food. It was like not going to bars to avoid the temptation to get drunk. I could avoid food completely. The problem came after the diet when I was supposed to start eating again. I would gain back all the weight I'd lost plus more within the first week. I think that I actually got fatter faster!

Then there were the extreme exercise programs. I was going to get skinny and in shape at the same time. That would have been great except that exercise made me hungrier, if that was even possible. I got stronger, but definitely not skinnier. Discouraged, I would just quit.

Food made me feel better emotionally. It filled an empty place inside, even if that feeling only lasted for a minute or two. I realized I had a huge problem when I stopped caring if the food even tasted good. I caught myself bingeing on food that I didn't even like. Why? Why couldn't I stop stuffing myself with food that didn't even taste good?

I'd been ridiculously skinny my whole life. I was almost six feet tall and had only weighed one hundred and eighteen pounds before this crazy addiction. How could this be happening to me? Why couldn't I control these urges?

It was hard to stop an addiction that I couldn't get away from. Drugs, alcohol, smoking— you could just avoid the people and places where those things were available, right? But I couldn't just stop eating forever, or I would die!

I started asking God about it. *God, why can't I control this? Why don't I ever feel full? I'm getting so ugly. Please help me change.*

Over the next few weeks, I read about the misconception Americans have about beauty and body image. I read that God created us in His image, so we were always beautiful. I heard people talk about accepting ourselves as God had made us. I read about different men liking different types of women. Some men even liked larger women. That was a shock!

God had designed every type of female figure. My perspective was out of whack. Maybe I needed to change how I saw myself. My way of seeing things was causing me more and more problems. How did I need to change to get different results?

You need to eat and exercise to be healthy, not to look a certain way. You need to thank Me for who I made you, regardless of how that looks. I created you exactly the way you need to be for My plan for your life. Trust me. I heard God say to my spirit.

So, of course, I argued. *I need to be skinny. No one will ever love me if I am fat!*

But your boyfriend rejected you when you were skinny, He replied. That was true.

I realized that my way of seeing life and my way of handling food were not working. I went back and forth between trusting God and wanting the look of a model. Finally, I gave in to God.

Ok God. I will thank you for how you designed me, even if that means I'm fluffy. I will eat and exercise to be healthy. I will no longer diet for appearances' sake. I will do my best to be healthy and thank You for how I look. Please help me to be grateful for the food you provide.

God, I will not count calories or fat grams any more. I will eat an adult portion of whatever food is available. I will not binge or snack outside of regular meals. Please, help me to be grateful. I promise to never diet for appearances' sake again.

My next meal was not low calorie. It had a moderate amount of meat, starch and vegies. I thanked God and ate everything that was put on my plate. For the first time in six months, I felt full. I forgot to snack because I didn't even think about food until I was called to the next meal at my cousin's house. When I ate that meal, I was full again. That felt wonderful.

Over the next six months, I ate regular food in moderate portions. I exercised a little, but I didn't go to extremes. I lost fifteen pounds. Since I had quit looking to scales for my value, I didn't even realize what was happening until my clothes started fitting differently. I just kept thanking God for how He had made me.

This happened almost thirty years ago. Since that time, I have gotten married and had five pregnancies. I have ranged in size between a four and a twelve. My weight has fluctuated, but I have kept thanking God for who and how He made me. He has always kept me feeling full at the end of reasonable meals. He has always provided the clothes I needed for whatever size I was at the time.

I have never felt the addiction pulling me to binge since I promised God I wouldn't diet for appearances' sake. Since that year, I've been so grateful that I haven't had to experience that horrible, empty, craving feeling that could never be satisfied. God's love has filled that empty place in me that food could never fill.

Praise ye the Lord. Praise God in his sanctuary: praise him in the firmament of his power. Praise him for his mighty acts: praise him according to his excellent greatness. Praise him with the sound of the trumpet: praise him with the psaltery and harp.

Praise him with the timbrel and dance: praise him with stringed instruments and organs.
Praise him upon the loud cymbals: praise him upon the high sounding cymbals.
Let every thing that hath breath praise the Lord. Praise ye the Lord.

Psalm 150

Living With War

By Nasturtium

Tears cascading down my face
I watch my man marching off to war
He stands so proud and tall
As he answers the call

To protect the weak and downtrodden
To defend our nation's freedom
To support his troops

I smile through the tears
And keep waving long after he's gone
Not wanting to turn and face
My life alone for a year

Patriotism won't keep me warm at night
Loyalty can't laugh at my jokes
Valor doesn't show affection

I will strive to be brave
I will smile on our rare calls
I tell myself that our love is worth it all
We are just doing our part

Independence requires fighting
Freedom calls for sacrifice
Liberty isn't free

Finally the day came
To embrace my strong, weary warrior
Who had fought bravely for us all
and survived so many battles

His body was whole and strong
His soul was battered
His spirit broken

Terrors he could still see
Nightmares making him scream in the night
Danger still haunting his reality
Loss permeating his days

Survivor's guilt making him feel unworthy
Survivor's hell tormenting his mind
Survivor's medals reminding

I know he wants to protect
Yet he explodes in anger
Trying so desperately to keep us safe
From anything that could harm

Wars against communism to win freedom
Wars against all terrorists to win safety
Wars against "whom" to win "what"

Disillusionment destroys from the inside
Stealing his purpose in life
Replacing it with anything
That dulls or distracts from the war within

Controlling the outcome of every single thing
Restricting his loved one's freedom
Forcing everyone to comply

God, please help me love
This broken man who is breaking me
Instill Your forgiveness in us both
As we navigate these stormy seas

Nurturing life to replace the death
Believing in hope and healing
Loving the unlovable

Surviving the war he went to fight
and the war he brought home inside
That's caused damage in ways
I'll never understand

Loving the husband who once believed
Forgiving him for his harsh cynicism
Praying for unshakeable faith

Years and wars have passed
Children have joined our ranks
Hello's have matched every goodbye
Our family stands together against all odds

Choosing to love God first and then each other
Having faith that God's plan is always best
Making the most of each day together

We Will Win This War!

Living With War:
a Participant's Commentary

Tears cascading down my face
I watch my man marching off to war
He stands so proud and tall
As he answers the call

*I want to be strong, I want it to be over, but now it is
time to roll.
He has a job that needs to be done. I have to be strong
and do my part.*

To protect the weak and downtrodden
To defend our nation's freedom
To support his troops

*We military families have our own views of war.
Mainly, we take it as being our husbands'/wives' jobs
and something that must be done--regardless of who we
are protecting, and even, in some cases, against our
beliefs.*

I smile through the tears
And keep waving long after he's gone
Not wanting to turn and face
My life alone for a year

I used to be alone, but now that I have children, we all go into survival mode. The tears stop. Whether we want to face it or not, the waiting inevitably starts. Now my main focus is keeping our children's lives as normal as possible while he's gone.

Patriotism won't keep me warm at night
Loyalty can't laugh at my jokes
Valor doesn't show affection

I will strive to be brave
I will smile on our rare calls
I tell myself that our love is worth it all
We are just doing our part

You nailed it here!

Independence requires fighting
Freedom calls for sacrifice
Liberty isn't free

Instead I would write:
As my faith keeps me going,
I battle my own fears,
I pray that the dreaded visit
with unimaginably bad news never arrives
We just have to make it to the end,
THEN everything will be alright
(or so I used to believe)

Finally the day came
To embrace my strong, weary warrior
Who had fought bravely for us all
and survived so many battles

His body was whole and strong
His soul was battered
His spirit broken

*I can't see the damage, but I can feel it. Slowly, I
realize that EVERY
THING is **NOT** alright, as I thought it would be. I don't
dare ask, but little by little I learn of the horrors that he
had to face. I wonder if he will ever be the same. The
kids ask, "Why is he so different? Why is he upset?" I
want to keep looking for the man that left a year ago. I
don't see that man, but looking in the mirror, I don't
see the same woman either. She has changed her
priorities, her wants, her needs, and her goals in life.
She is just happy that war is over for her family, for
now. But she's sad that war has entered her home. She
sees her children and knows that they somehow also
know that the man who loves them so much is hurting
in ways we can only imagine.*

Terrors he could still see
Nightmares making him scream in the night
Danger still haunting his reality
Loss permeating his days

Survivor's guilt making him feel unworthy
Survivor's hell tormenting his mind
Survivor's medals reminding

*He remembers that those medals were given to the
survivors instead of to the ones who gave their lives.*

I know he wants to protect
Yet he explodes in anger
Trying so desperately to keep us safe
From anything that could harm

Wars against communism to win freedom
Wars against all terrorists to win safety
Wars against "whom" to win "what"

*Was it worth it? Did it matter? It mattered to us.
Perhaps we are only numbers, and numbers that don't
count as casualties because we were the "fortunate"
ones that got our soldier back alive. It mattered to us
because we know that something died on both fronts,
and we have to face our new reality.*

Disillusionment destroys from the inside
Stealing his purpose in life
Replacing it with anything
That dulls or distracts from the war within

Controlling the outcome of every single thing
Restricting his loved one's freedom
Forcing everyone to comply

God, please help me love
This broken man who is breaking me
Instill Your forgiveness in us both
As we navigate these stormy seas

*God, please give me the strength and wisdom to
overcome every crisis, to make the best of what we have
left. I know this man didn't mean to bring war into our
home. Together we must force war back out.*

Nurturing life to replace the death
Believing in hope and healing
Loving the unlovable

Surviving the war he went to fight
and the war he brought home inside
That's caused damage in ways
I'll never understand

*….and I don't want to understand. Despite our new
reality, we can say that we are not victims but
survivors. As survivors, we will look for new tomorrows
because, no matter what, we made it through. Thank
you God he didn't come back inside a "black bag."
With Your help, we will take care of the "black bag"
that he brought back with him.*

Loving the husband who once believed
Forgiving him for his harsh cynicism
Praying for unshakeable faith

Years and wars have passed
Children have joined our ranks
Hello's have matched every goodbye
Our family stands together against all odds.

*Whenever we watch people fight over trivial things, we
roll our eyes because we are fighting a battle that must
continue to be fought. War took so much from us, but
there is also so much ahead of us, and for that we are
eternally grateful.*

Choosing to love God first and then each other
Having faith that God's plan is always best
Making the most of each day together

This is the best stanza!

We Will Win This War!

Dear Anne,

Dear Anne,

I wanted to write you this letter to explain
how I felt when you repeatedly shut me
out when I wanted to help you. I wanted to
be there for you during difficult times. You
kept telling me that I didn't understand what
you were going through. You know, you were
right. I didn't understand.

No one can ever fully understand what
someone else is going through even if they
have gone through something similar
themselves. For a long time I couldn't
understand why you would shut me out
after all that we'd been through together.

Do you remember how you used to stick up
for me when mom would blame me for

things that Julie had done? You got into
more trouble trying to keep me from getting
blamed unjustly! You were my big sister and
I looked up to you. Then you became a
teenager. I was still in elementary school.

You shut me out because you wanted to
hang out with the older kids. At the time, I
thought you were rejecting me, but I realize
now that you were just trying to grow up
and be your own person.

The next year, when I was a teenager, too.
You started talking to me again. As teenagers
we realized that we had some things in
common that we would rather not have
experienced. We were both raped as children
and suffered the added trauma of holding it
all in and not telling anyone. We both felt
that we couldn't trust adults to keep us
safe and therefore turned to God as the only
one who we could count on.

God gave us a special bond, and I thought
that we would always be there for each
other no matter what. That's what made it
hurt so badly when your husband told me

that I couldn't have any contact with you
because, he said, I was repeatedly hurting
you. If I wanted to tell you something, he
said that it had to go through him.

I did not know what I had done to hurt you
so badly.

As far as I knew, our relationship was
close, with a lot of give and take. I helped
you with house cleaning and childcare. You
lent me your timeshare so that my family
could go on vacations and helped me take
care of things that I wasn't comfortable
handling myself. Sure, we fought sometimes,
but we always forgave each other and made
up right away.

I was so hurt that you had sent your
husband to tell me there was a problem
rather than telling me yourself. I didn't
understand. It was years before I realized
that when he prohibited our talking, your
husband was isolating you from your
support system.

We could talk about anything, and he was afraid that I might figure out that he was emotionally abusing you.

When we finally talked again, you explained that you had never meant to reject me. We forgave each other and loved each other despite the years of crossed signals and feelings of rejection on both sides. Once again, we were able to help each other out.

I was with you when you found out that your husband was back in contact with the "other woman" that he had sworn to never speak to again. Instead of going on a date night with my husband, I held you as you cried. Your husband had sworn that he would never do to his children what his father had done to him – yet he did. You were devastated. I was too.

When you got a divorce, my husband and I were there for you and helped you in every way we knew how. We took care of your children many evenings and weekends when you had to work. That year was especially hard for me because you kept telling me that

I didn't understand what you were going through. You were right again.

I didn't realize that you couldn't handle seeing me suffer for you. You could barely handle life with your own pain. Seeing me suffer with you put you into big sister mode. Taking care of both of us was more than you could handle.

All I knew was that I kept trying to include you with our family to let you know that you were loved – but you kept running away. During Thanksgiving that first year you went to the beach – alone – rather than spend the time with us, your family. I know that you said that your counselor told you to get away, but Thanksgiving is our most important family holiday.

When I talked to you about it, you just kept saying that you had no family. That hurt me more than anything. How could you say that? I knew that your kids were with their dad, but we were still here. I didn't understand that being around all of us just drove home what you had lost. It was like salt in a wound. Our love couldn't compensate for the pain that the holiday would cause you. I'm sorry that I didn't understand.

I took it personally when you missed my children's birthday parties. They missed you. You have always been an important part of their lives. I had made such an effort to be there for your children after the divorce. It hurt that my children didn't seem important to you. I didn't understand that being around happy families was like reopening a wound. You needed time to heal.

Then your life took a nosedive. Your "perfect" job turned into a nightmare of epic proportions. You were working 70 to 80 hours a week. You were facing awful choices that I had never had to face. Once again I didn't understand. I was still there to listen when you wanted to talk, to love you and to pray.

Praying helped me. I could pray for you when I didn't understand what you were going through because I knew that He did.

When you couldn't open up and talk to me, I
know that you opened up and talked to Him
because that's who you always went to
when you were hurting.

The time came when you started running
from God. That was so hard for me to
watch. I wanted to help you, shield you, and
protect you like you used to do for me. But
you just kept saying that I didn't
understand.

You already knew all the things that I was
trying to tell you about making good choices,
I know. I probably just sounded preachy to
you at the time, and so you started to avoid
me, too. That really hurt! I felt so
helpless. You were headed toward a cliff, and
I couldn't stop you. I kept forgetting that
I didn't have to. God had you in His hand in
the midst of your darkest time.

I've learned to forgive right away when I
hear those words "You don't understand,"
because I don't. I now know that you never
meant to hurt me. You were often so
caught up in your own pain and in just

making it through the next five minutes that you were incapable of processing how your words came across to me. How they made me feel wasn't even on your radar.

Whether I understand or not is ultimately not the point. All God wants me to do is be there for you. I can listen when you want to talk and pray for you when you don't. I can help you when I know that there is a need.

Thank you for the times that you have been there for me, too. When I had the miscarriage you cried with me, listened to me and prayed with me. You have made it possible for my husband and me to have countless date nights. You have passed along clothes for my children and bought me clothes, too. Thank you for all of the lessons - good and bad - that I've gotten to learn by watching you, instead of having to go through those experiences myself.

I have been encouraged by seeing where your journey has finally led you. You missed that cliff that I was worried about, and now you are passing out maps to help other people avoid some of the perils that you faced. God has been so good to us.

Luke 4:18 is such a great reminder of what God wants each of us to do: "The Spirit of the Lord is upon me, because he... hath sent me to heal the brokenhearted... to set at liberty them that are bruised." Thank you for your patience with me. God had lessons for both of us to learn through the experiences that He has taken us through.

I am thankful that you are my sister two times over – we have the same parents and we serve the same God. With His help and each other's support we can make it through anything!

Love you Sis,
Night-blooming Jasmine

*Great is the Lord, and greatly to be praised in the city
of our God, in the mountain of his holiness.
Beautiful for situation, the joy of the whole earth, is
mount Zion, on the sides of the north, the city of the
great King.
God is known in her palaces for a refuge.*

Psalm 48: 1-3

Conclusion:

My Light on the Hill is a Pile of Burning $#;+!

Standing outside my home in the dark, I was asking God why I had to go through such messy, stinky, horrible things. Why did my story of being redeemed have to start with shame and guilt? I knew I was supposed to be a light to others. I was not supposed to "hide under a bushel." I wanted to have a testimony to help others.

I wanted to be a lighthouse, warning others of danger. I had always loved lighthouses. I'd started collecting them in college. I had a lamp that was a beautiful lighthouse with roses growing up the sides of it. I had lighthouses that were every size and color. I decorated my library in lighthouses. The small bathroom looked so pretty with lighthouses in clean, crisp blue and white. Lighthouses represented stability, safety, beauty, direction, outreach.

Like a lighthouse, I wanted to be "built on a rock that couldn't be shaken." I wanted to stand out as a bright light in a dark world — pointing others to

Christ. I wanted to lead by example. Show others how to follow Christ the "right" way.

Yet, here I was agonizing over the darkest, ugliest, messiest situation I'd ever experienced. I was horrified. I was crying out to God because I couldn't talk to anyone else about this latest nightmare.

God, how can I ever help anyone else when my own life is so messed up? I feel like I've just had the fiftieth dump truck of manure dumped on my head. I'm living in the middle of a fertilizer processing center. Everything stinks! How will I ever be able to help anyone else? What happened to my calling to ministry? I feel like crap!

I wasn't trying to sound proper or religious. I was devastated and angry. I was raw, broken, and afraid. There was no way for anything good to come out of any of this mess. That's when I pictured a huge pile of manure on top of a hill. Yep, that was me. Nothing pretty about it. It needed to be burned to the ground.

Then, I saw it catch fire. Small flames grew until the whole thing was a raging fire. Wait a second; that wasn't a normal fire. It was beautiful! All the things that made it ugly and stinky also made it burn with the colors of the rainbow. It was the most beautiful fire I'd ever seen.

That's your testimony! That's what I want you to share with others--quietly settled into my spirit.

I quit crying and just stood there. A serene peace settled over me. I did have a testimony to share. I wasn't the only one who was broken. Others would need to know that God can carry you through anything. God can redeem you out of any situation. We like the promise that He will give us "beauty for ashes," but we don't want to admit to the mess that has to get burned to create those ashes.

The stories you've just read are from women of different colors, from different backgrounds, from different economic levels, and from different places across the country. Evil doesn't just target one type of girl or woman. Anyone can be a victim. We are just sharing a sampling of the nightmares that God has carried us through.

He says He will never leave us nor forsake us. Be honest with Him about your need for help. Be real. I promise He will meet you in whatever hell you are in. God will walk you through it. You can become an Ex-Victim whose testimony can help other "victims".

Heaven and earth shall pass away, but my words shall not pass away.

Matthew 24:35

Next Steps

By Rose

If the pages of this book have opened up for you an understanding of the pain that someone you care for deeply has endured, it has served its purpose well. If you have waded through this field of flowers - watering it with your tears, use your growing awareness and deepening insights. Connect more openly with the people in your life who you know have experienced pain that you are only now beginning to fathom. If you know that they are still in the rocky place...still facing a gaping black hole of absolute desperation and hopelessness...help them see that hole as a place where a flower can grow.

There are several universal truths to bear in mind – regardless of race, gender, religion or age:

- God is good.
- You are loved.
- We are in this together.

Don't forget to.....
- Be thankful.
- Choose life.
- Treat your body like the temple that it is.
- Be honest with yourself and others.
- We are in this together.
- Focus on what you want more of – not what you fear.

If you stepped on stage in solidarity with the little naked girl as you read these personal narratives, was your heart linked with hers? If so, your hands can now stretch out to help others – sharing the reality that they are not alone. Healing, life, and love are available and to be embraced.

Share these with a "Victim" during her recovery time:

1. You're not alone

2. It's not your fault – don't beat yourself up

3. You are loved

4. There is hope after this

5. Forgive yourself and forgive the person that hurt and abused you– Forgiveness does not mean the thing that happened was right but it sets you free from the person who harmed you.

Did I mention that YOU ARE LOVED!

EX-VICTIM

By Zinnia

I don't **want** to admit I'm a "Victim"
Tainted by abuse
Feeling irrational fear and shame
Defensive and jaded
Frigid, stoic, rude
Rejecting before I get rejected

I don't want to **admit** I'm a "Victim"
Who was too weak
To get away, to fight, to stop the pain
To stand up to the bully
Who killed my innocence
Who massacred my soul

I don't want to *be* the "Victim"
Making mistakes
That cause more abuse
Broken choices that hurt me
I end up hurting others
Instead of stopping the pain

I want to *stop* being a "Victim"
Attracting predators
Accepting abuse as my due
Putting myself at risk
Choosing to trust the wrong ones
Who just pretend to protect

Jesus, *help* me stop being a "Victim"
You became a victim for me
You hung naked on the cross
You bore my shame
You were bruised for my iniquities
By Your stripes, I am healed

I am *no longer* a "Victim"
Forgiven of sin
With wholeness of heart
Redeemed, healed and loved
My innocence restored
My soul saved

I am *now* an "Ex-Victim"
I testify of His grace
I was lost but am found
I was shattered but am restored
I am filled with relentless love
I am sharing it with others just like me

*Beloved, let us **love** one another: for **love is** of **God**; and every one that **love**th **is** born of **God**, and knoweth **God**.*

1 John 4:7

Dear Reader,

Dear Reader,

     Yesterday, I went hiking with my three boys and had so much fun. We ran and climbed everything climbable. We hugged trees and danced on rocks. We chased each other and hid from each other. We took turns giving and getting piggyback rides. We are a wonderful team, but we have not always been that way.

     I was depressed and hated being a mom. I was too damaged to be a fun part of my kids' lives. I loved my boys, but in a distant way that worked as long as I didn't have to spend too much time with them. Now, as a homeschooling, single mom, I spend 24/7 with them and love every minute of it. There is a process in getting damaged; there is also a process in getting healed.

     You know my story was mixed in with the anonymous stories you've just read. I was motivated to write this book because I know what it's like to be in a dark place—too hurt and ashamed to reach out for help. Dark places are not easy things to live through. They are not easy to get past. But with God's grace, I did get past my abuse.

I not only survived, but healed. I'm a walking testimony of God's power to heal and restore. My sons are stable, loving, friendly children. I give God all the credit for survival, healing and restoration.

You can move forward. You can get out of your own darkness. If you haven't been in a dark place yourself, this may give you glimpses into helping someone else get out of her darkness. I am not a trained counselor or minister, but I do know God's miraculous saving grace.

No matter what anyone else has told you, God loves you! I'm not talking about "religion" or a "higher power," I'm talking about a loving Creator who designed us in His image. He loves us and wants nothing more than to have us reach out to Him for love and redemption

Even as a Christian, I had to recognize that I had a problem and needed help. That might have been really obvious to others, but it took a while for me to admit it to myself. I didn't know I was actually depressed until my two-year-old drew simple faces of all his family in his daycare. He had all the family members with smiles, except mine. I was frowning. That hurt like crazy.

It woke me up to the fact that I was depressed and not hiding it very well. I knew I cried a lot, but I thought it wasn't affecting anyone else. I thought I was hiding it from everyone, everyone except my two-year-old, evidently.

I had traumas, problems and fears. I needed God's help. I did not get His help until I was willing to admit I had a problem. Then, I had to ask Him to help me. Not only admit, but I had to be willing to do what I needed to do to heal. In my case, there was a lot of damage. Healing was a long process. I want to share with you some of the process to give you hope. God can, and will, meet you, too.

After asking God to provide the right people to help and support me, I started asking for help. God used a variety of ministries including Celebrate Recovery, Be In Health™, Christian counseling, and the prayers of family and friends. There is no shame in being too weak to make it on your own. The Bible says that in our weakness, God is made strong. I couldn't become an Ex-Victim without first admitting I was a victim.

Abuse set me up to make bad choices that made me even more of a victim. Getting help to understand the cycle and how to stop it has changed my life. I do NOT have to stay a victim. In Christ, I can be whole. There isn't a magic formula for this. It is a journey of healing.

God has miraculously healed some areas of damage. Healing in other areas has been a very slow process. I try not to judge myself by where I am in my healing. Instead, I ask God to continue the process until I am completely healed.

I've also had to face the fact that healing doesn't always look like I want it to. I'd prefer to just erase the bad things as if they had never happened. I'd like to forget the pain. Instead, I've realized that healing means that the pain can no longer hurt me or my future.

I still feel pain when I go back to revisit my dark places. In fact, I've had to do that a lot as I've written these stories. Writing other people's stories has brought my own pain back to the surface. The miracle is that it can no longer damage me.

Forgiving has been the most important part of my healing. I was a prisoner of bitterness, which kept me from moving forward in any area. On my own, I was definitely not strong enough to forgive anyone else, much less forgive myself. I asked God to help me forgive. This was not an emotional thing. Forgiving was a deliberate choice that had to be followed by praying for the person who had hurt me.

Corrie ten Boom was my example of forgiveness. She forgave her guards, who had horribly abused her and her family at a concentration camp during WWII. Forgiving the person who'd hurt me didn't let that person off the hook; it just freed me to heal. Then, I had to forgive myself. This was harder, but more life changing.

I now have the ability to feel a very broad spectrum of emotions. Just as I have felt excruciating pain, I can now feel unbelievable joy! Just as little things can trigger memories of dark times, little things can trigger feelings of happiness. I don't ever want to go back to the numb stage where denial and walls blocked me from feeling anything! I want to feel life's ups and downs without letting those feelings control or define me.

I have my own little ways of brightening up my life. I surround myself with positive, joyful, worshipful music. I have positive quotes and scriptures on my walls. I have pictures and paintings on my walls that trigger warm, safe, happy feelings. I read scripture daily to feed my spirit life. I avoid too much emotional junk food. Since a lot of entertainment leaves me sad or depressed, music, movies, and books that might leave me feeling bad are not on my regular menu.

I "stop to smell the roses" whenever I see them. I pause to look at the funny looking clouds, gorgeous sunsets, and bright rainbows. I ask God to show me the beauty and joy around me. Sometimes it's just the little flower growing in the cracked sidewalk. Sometimes it's just the smile on someone's face. Sometimes it's a joke I read or hear. Sometimes it's just knowing God really does love me.

God has also pointed out some key principles that help me make better choices when I may be confused by my past damage. These are my 5 T's:

TEMPLE: The Bible says I am God's temple here on earth. That means He created me as someone with value and beauty. It means that I'm designed for worshiping Him. It means I need to cherish and protect my temple from anything or anyone that would desecrate or dishonor it. I'm so thankful that God will cleanse my temple anytime I ask Him to. I need to make healthy choices about food and exercise to keep my temple in the best possible shape. I recognize that He designed my temple the way He wanted it to be. My job is to do my best to take care of it so it can honor my Creator. When I mess up, I just ask Him to help me do better moving forward.

TEAM: I can't do this alone. I need Jesus and the Holy Spirit to help me. I also need my family, friends, and spending time with others talking about God and worshiping Him. My team includes my children. My team also includes a Christian counselor. I also asked God, and He gave me Godly people who would love me and pray for me consistently. I'm at my weakest when I'm isolated from my team. Thankfully, I always have access to my Savior.

TEMPERANCE: This means I need to choose self-control and balance in my life. Extremes can often cause damage. I need to put measures in place that help me make good choices. If something is a temptation, I can make choices to limit my exposure to that. I can ration treats instead of bingeing. There is no balance or control in addictions. If something is starting to control me, I need to reevaluate what I'm doing and get help.

TRUTH: I need to be honest with God, with myself, and with others. Lies usually do more damage to the person telling them than they do to the person hearing them. Denial is a lie that protects us temporarily, but eventually it does even more harm. Covering up damage and wounds can make them fester and get worse. I had to be very careful where I went to get help. When God directed me, I was safe and could share the complete truth. Honesty got me the help I needed to heal and change.

THANKFULNESS: The Bible says "in everything give thanks." I've found out that I can't be depressed and thankful at the same time. If I'm actively giving thanks, I'm not focusing on the bad, but on the good. Sometimes the only things I could find to be thankful for were that I was still alive or that Jesus died on the cross for me. Sometimes it's been that I've gotten to eat or sleep on a bed. Sometimes it's been that my boys are alive. It can be a tough job to find something to be thankful for when our world has crashed around us or when we see nothing but darkness and pain. I know. I also know that thanking God has always lifted my spirit.
Every day I am thankful that I have an opportunity to start fresh.

I'm so grateful that you have read this book. My greatest desire for you is that you have renewed hope. I pray for each person who finds themselves reading this book. I ask God to reveal Himself to you in the stories shared here.

Each woman shared her story praying that her testimony would bring hope and life to you. We are all flowers who have learned to *Bloom In the Dark*. We are all praying for complete healing and restoration for you through a relationship with Jesus Christ. Then you too can *Bloom In the Dark!*

In Christ's love,
Paula

PS. A couple of books that really helped me were:
A More Excellent Way by Dr. Henry Wright
One Thousand Gifts by Ann Voskamp
Jesus Today by Sarah Young
90 Days of God's Goodness by Randy Alcorn

Recommendations from a Christian Counselor:

The first step to locating a good, Christian counselor is to use the Samaritan Institute website at http://www.samaritaninstitute.org. This is a network of Christian counseling centers that can provide the needed counseling or refer to someone who can.

There are several authors and books that can help, although there isn't a book or author that I've recommended that is specifically a survivor of sexual rather than other forms of abuse.

With that preface, I would suggest:

- Chonda Pierce, a Christian comedian and in particular her book:

  Laughing in the Dark: A Comedian's Journey Through Depression

- Sheila Walsh, a Christian speaker and singer and in particular her book:

  Loved Back to Life: How I Found the Courage to Live Free

- Henry Cloud and John Townsend have a series of books that are strong:

Boundaries

- Another "classic" in this area is Melody Beattie's book:

Codependent No More

- Robert McGee's combined book and workbook for people who want or need a structured tool for healing and wholeness in Christ:

The Search for Significance

Also, I sometimes suggest **Celebrate Recovery**, which is a Christian 12-step ministry both for people with addictions of all kinds and for people who struggle with codependency due to abuse of all kinds. In reality, most victims of abuse tend to struggle with addictions, so Celebrate Recovery is helpful from multiple directions.

Acknowledgements

First, I want to thank each woman who was willing to go back to her black hole to share her pain and healing for the benefit of countless others. From all across the country, you have reached out to me to share your testimony. This book is a labor of love. To give others hope, each of you stood on stage with me and exposed your deepest pain. You've shared secrets you'd never told anyone before.

Thank you for helping me accomplish my mission of providing a tool that will give hope to those walking through darkness. Thank you for your vulnerability and transparency. On behalf of every little girl and woman looking for a sign that she can make it through her nightmare, THANK YOU.

Also, thank you to those who offered stories not included in this book. Each story touched my heart. Please keep sharing your testimony with others. I'm hoping I will get to work with you and others to share more testimonies in the future.

A special thank-you to my three, amazing, homeschooled sons. You boys have helped cook, do laundry, clean, and anything else I needed done so I could do my writing. You entertained each other and helped each other with homework.

Bryan, thank you for doing your schoolwork so consistently without being micromanaged. You've finished each chore with excellence. Justin, thank you for finishing your schoolwork efficiently so you could make lunch every day. You've been a huge help in giving me the time I needed to work. Will, thank you for keeping such a good attitude when I wasn't available to you all the time. Your hugs and laughter have brightened every day.

Boys, I could never have finished this book without your love and support. I thank God every day for you. And, no, you may not read this book until you are eighteen.

Thank you to my incredible, extended family. Each one of you has supported me in this endeavor. You have prayed, encouraged and blessed me in so many ways. If you thought I was crazy for writing a book instead of having a "real job," you didn't let on. Instead, you went out of your way to help this dream become a reality. From financial support to editing and feedback on stories, you each have played an important role. I'd name all of you if I didn't have such a huge family!

Mom and Dad, thank you for all your prayers and encouragement. This was a very emotional journey. Knowing that you were praying for me, reading and editing the stories, and cheering me on helped immensely. You have set an example of following God at all costs. From the mission field to the business arena, you have stayed true to your beliefs. Thank you for the Christian heritage you passed down.

Thank you to Nancy Duke Mitchell for painting the cover of the book. You've shared your talent to bless others. May your art continue to glorify God!

Thank you to Nancy Lott with Nancy Lott Photography for the author picture. The pictures you took helped me realize how far I had come in my healing journey. I felt like I was seeing myself through my heavenly Father's eyes.

Thank you to Carmen Gloria Ore for your beautiful vision expressed in the logos and book cover. Your talent in graphic design is amazing. Your passion for Christ is undeniable!

Thank you, also, to the countless others who have contributed in various ways to this book. God knows who you are and will bless you.

This book has been a miracle in the making. I think I could write a book about writing this book and all the ways God stepped in to make this happen. He directed me to coordinate this project and work with the most amazing people in putting it together.

Father God, His Son Jesus, and His Holy Spirit are the most important reality in my life and in the lives of the people who teamed up for this book.

Thank You, God, for changing my life. Thank You for the personal healing that has made this book possible. All of the honor and glory are Yours.

Contact

I would love to hear how God has walked you through your dark places. If you don't know Christ, I'd like to encourage you to find Him.

If you've been healed and restored, I'd like to share your story to encourage others. If you just want encouragement, please join us in one of these ways:

www.bloominthedark.com

www.facebook.com/bloominthedark

www.pinterest.com/bloominthedark/

https://twitter.com/bloominthedark

bloominthedarkbook@gmail.com

"...whatsoever things are true, whatsoever things are honest, whatsoever things are just, whatsoever things are pure, whatsoever things are lovely, whatsoever things are of good report; if there be any virtue, and if there be any praise, think on these things."
Philippians 4:8

About the Author

Born in the jungles of Peru to missionary parents, Paula's beginning in life was anything but typical. Separated from her family for six months at the age of 3, she learned about abandonment and abuse very early. For as long as she can remember, she has had to depend on God.

Raped at the age of 5, Paula was caught in a cycle of damage and abuse which lasted into her thirties. From sexual abuse to later mental, emotional and even spiritual abuse, Paula developed a victim mentality, which fueled decades of continued abuse. The trauma she experienced caused her to develop a variety of psychosomatic illnesses which, at times, left her bed-ridden.

Broken beyond endurance and suicidal, Paula cried out to God for help. He miraculously intervened, faithfully walking with her through a dramatic healing process. Along the way, Paula learned to stand up to her abusers and stop attracting predators. She now knows, from personal experience, the healing, deliverance, and hope that only God can bring.

Through the ministry of Bloom in The Dark, Paula focuses on writing and speaking to women—raising awareness about abuse, bringing hope to victims, and partnering with ministries to help women survive and thrive.

As a certified Life Coach, Paula can encourage women to move into a fullfiling future that is not defined by their past.

A single mom living in Nashville, Paula homeschools her three sons, ranging in age from six to fourteen. The boys are a key part of Paula's support team and her biggest fans. Together they enjoy swimming, hiking and roller skating.

To contact Paula, go to www.bloominthedark.com.

Business Blooms Partners
THANK YOU!

BalancingHealthHQ.com
Linda Goetze
(478) 955-7649

Project4:8

Digital Logos
Branding
Artwork
& More

Draw near to God and he will draw near to you

Carmen Ruiz-Ore
407-353-6566
carmen.ruiz-ore@outlook.com

Doing GOD's work Digitally

Serenity University
Christian Life Coaching by Ginny Priz
serenityuniversity.com | (908)507-9256

~~Overwhelm~~	~~Fear~~	✓ Courses	✓ Practical Exercises
~~Anxiety~~	~~Shame~~	✓ Coaching	✓ Confidentiality
~~Guilt~~	~~Codependency~~	✓ Biblical Wisdom	✓ Peer Support

Finally Acheive Freedom from Negative Emotions